AF608191

THE CATHOLIC UNIVERSITY OF AMERICA
CANON LAW STUDIES
No. 195

THE EXAMINATION OF THE QUALITIES OF THE ORDINAND

AN HISTORICAL SYNOPSIS AND COMMENTARY

BY

THOMAS RAPHAEL GALLAGHER, O.P., A.B., S.T.LR., J.C.D.

Priest of the Province of St. Joseph

A DISSERTATION

Submitted to the Faculty of the School of Canon Law of the Catholic University of America in Partial Fulfillment of the Requirements for the Degree of Doctor of Canon Law

THE CATHOLIC UNIVERSITY OF AMERICA PRESS
WASHINGTON, D. C.
1944

REVISORES ORDINIS:

EDUARDUS C. DALY, O.P., S.T.M.
PAULUS A. SKEHAN, O.P., S.T.LR., J.C.D.

IMPRIMI POTEST:

TERENTIUS S. MCDERMOTT, O.P., S.T.LR., LL.D.,
Prior Provincialis.

Neo-Eboraci, die 22 *aug.* 1944.

NIHIL OBSTAT:

EDUARDUS ROELKER, S.T.D., J.C.D.,
Censor Deputatus.

Washingtonii, die 29 *aprilis* 1944.

IMPRIMATUR:

✠ MICHAEL J. CURLEY, D.D.,
Archiepiscopus Baltimorensis et Washingtonensis.

Baltimore, die 29 *aprilis* 1944.

Printed by
The Rosary Press
Somerset, Ohio

IN
MEMORY
OF
KEVIN

TABLE OF CONTENTS

FOREWORD

In writing to Timothy St. Paul instructs him: "Do not lay hands hastily upon anyone, and do not be a partner in other men's sins."[1] Through the centuries this apostolic admonition is constantly in the mind of the Church, urging Her to exercise care in the selection and training of those aspiring to the sacred ministry. She is eminently desirous both of insuring the presence of the necessary qualities in the ordinand and of avoiding the harm done to souls by those destitute of a divine vocation, yet presumptuous to the extent of seeking ordination. To achieve this purpose certain basic norms receive attention early in the history of ecclesiastical legislation. Later they are supplemented by decrees more specific in character and precisely adapted to the requirements of particular periods. All these norms, particularly as enunciated in c. 5, D. XXIV of the *Decretum Gratiani,* the title *De scrutinio in ordine faciendo* of the *Decretales Gregorii IX,* the legislation of the Council of Trent, canons 993-1000 of the Code of Canon Law, and the recent instructions of the Holy See, coalesce to provide material for this study.

The purpose of the dissertation is not so much the analysis of the various qualities required of ordinands as a consideration of the method of determining the presence or absence of these requisites. In the historical synopsis emphasis is placed on Decretal and Tridentine legislation as focal points, but the manner of procedure and reference indicates the ultimate sources of the various enactments. The canonical commentary is primarily concerned with canons 993-1000, but appropriate reference is also made to other norms pertinent to the study.

In the commencement, composition and completion of this work the writer has been the recipient of many favors. Particularly, he is grateful to the religious superiors whose permission and encouragement provided an opportunity for advanced study in Canon Law, to the Faculty of the School of Canon Law of the Catholic University of America for inspiration and direction, to his brethren of the Dominican House of Studies, Washington, D. C., for bearing so charitably with the inconveniences caused them by this study.

[1] 1 *Tim.* V, 22.

PART ONE
HISTORICAL SYNOPSIS

CHAPTER I
DECRETAL LAW

Article I. *Necessity and Subject of the Examination*

A. *Ordination of His Own Subject by the Bishop*

The first mention of an examination is in the legislation of the Third Council of Carthage (397). Gratian quotes this council as determining that "no one may be ordained a cleric unless he be approved by an examination of the bishops or by the testimony of the people."[1] This is the general norm and indicates that an examination prior to the reception of orders, unlike the scrutiny forming part of the actual ceremony of ordination, is not an absolute necessity, since its equivalent is found in an attestation of approval by the people.[2] In fact, such testimony is more important than an examination, since it is illicit for the bishop to ordain without at least consulting his clerics and seeking the approval of the people.[3]

This qualification of the necessity for an examination must be remembered if one is to avoid confusion when reading the commentators. When Ioannes Andreae († 1348) writes that "neither benefices nor orders are to be conferred without a diligent examination being made,"[4] he is to be understood, at least in the case of or-

[1] C. 2, D. XXIV—III Council of Carthage (397), cap. XXII—Mansi, *Sacrorum Conciliorum Nova et Amplissima Collectio* (53 vols. in 59, Paris, Leipzig, Arnhem, 1901-1927), III, 949.

[2] Ioannes Teutonicus, *Glossa Ordinaria,* ad c. 2, D. XXIV, v. *Testimonio.* Cf. Rufinus, *Summa Decretorum* (ed. Singer, Paderborn, 1902), D. XXIV.

[3] C. 6, D. XXIV—I Council of Constantinople (381)—Mansi, III, 593; c. 5, D. LI—IV Council of Toledo (633), cap. XIX—Mansi, X, 624.

[4] *In VI Libros Decretalium Novella Commentaria* (6 vols. in 5, Venetiis, 1581), tit. *de officio archidiaconi,* c. *Ad haec* (I, 23, 7).

ders, as meaning that suitability is not proved in the other manner possible, viz. by testimony of the people.

Furthermore, the bishop may dispense with the examination if the fitness of the candidate is already known to him. Only *ignoti*, "those whose origin, life and irregularity are unknown to the bishop,"[5] need undergo such a scrutiny.[6] St. Gregory the Great (590-604)[7] insists on this because so many of them are Manicheans and pretend they have minor orders. Later, St. Raymond († 1275)[8] elaborates further by declaring that they are "for the greater part criminals, infamous, excommunicated, or otherwise irregular. Also, they often lie, saying they have orders when they do not, or that they have more than they have."[9]

This interpretation is supported by other actions of St. Gregory.

[5] Raymundus de Pennafort, S., *Summa* (Veronae, 1744), III, t. 21, § 1.

[6] *Glossa,* ad c. 2, D. XXIV, v. *Testimonio:* noti non sunt examinandi: Sed tantum ignoti. Cf. c. 5, D. XXIV—Council of Nantes, cap. XI. This and other canons of the Council of Nantes are of uncertain origin. It was at one time thought that the Council had been celebrated around the years 658-660. Later study assigned these same decrees to a synod ca. 895-900. Recent critical study is inclined to link the canons of the Council of Nantes with others manufactured with the aid of 10th and 11th century compilers. Cf. Mansi, XVIII a, 169; *Acta Conciliorum et Epistolae Decretales ac Constitutiones Summorum Pontificum* (ed. Regia, 10 vols., Parisiis, 1714-1715), III, 985; *Lexicon für Theologie und Kirche* (10 vols., Freiburg im Breisgau: Herder, 1930-1938), VII, 438, v. "Nantes." C. 2, D. XLII—S. Ioannes Chrysostomus, *In Epistolam ad Hebraeos,* cap. VIII, homil. XII—Migne, *Patrologiae Cursus Completus, Series Graeca* (161 vols., Parisiis, 1856-1866), LXIII, 96; c. 5, D. LI—IV Council of Toledo (633), cap. XIX—Mansi, X, 624.

[7] C. 3, D. XCVIII—epist. *Pastoralis officii,* iul. 592—Jaffé *Regesta Pontificum Romanorum ab condita Ecclesia ad annum post Christum natum, 1198, Editionem secundam correctam et auctam auspiciis Gulielmi Wattenbach curaverunt S. Loewenfeld, F. Kaltenbrunner, P. Ewald* (2 vols. in 1, Lipsiae, 1885-1888), n. 1191.

[8] *Summa, loc. cit.*

[9] Cf. c. 1, X, *de clericis peregrinis,* I, 22—Alexander III (1159-1181), *Tua nos duxit*—Jaffé n. 13842; c. 2, X, *de clericis peregrinis,* I, 22—Innocentius III (1198-1216), *Inter quatuor animalia,* 2 aug. 1206—Potthast, *Regesta Pontificum Romanorum inde ab anno post Christum natum 1198 ad annum 1304* (2 vols., Berolini, 1874-1875), n. 2860.

The pontiff entrusts Sicily to a subdeacon[10] and Bishop Maximian[11] because their qualifications are known, and he demands an investigation into the charges of usury and foolishness brought against a certain Peter, a person unknown to the Holy Father but chosen by the people of Naples to be their archbishop.[12]

Innocent III (1198-1216)[13] proceeds in a similar manner by requiring a year of probation when certain knowledge is lacking concerning a monk. In this case the glossator notes the former custom of making a cleric *ignotus* and a laic *notus* spend two years on trial; a cleric *notus,* a year; and a laic *ignotus.,* three years.[14]

It is with these distinctions in mind that the necessity of an examination for all who wish to receive holy orders is to be understood. In a word, those candidates are exempted who are known to the bishop either personally or through the testimony of the faithful. Others, *ignoti* to both bishop and people, must be examined.

B. *Ordination of the Subject of Another*

When a candidate is sent for ordination from one bishop to another, there is a difficulty of which the commentators are not unaware. In considering the question Hostiensis († 1271) and Ioannes Andreae († 1348) emphasize slightly different aspects of the problem. The former is insisting on the necessity of the examination when he writes that "if anyone ordains a strange cleric at the mandate of another, he ought to examine him unless, for instance, the one commissioning him indicates that he has examined."[15] Hostiensis further notes that at the time of his writing this is not very well

[10] C. 1, D. XCIV—*Valde necessarium,* 3 sept. 590—Jaffé, n. 1067. Friedberg notes that Gratian erroneously attributes this letter to Pope Symmachus.

[11] C. 6, X, *de praesumptionibus, II, 23—Mandata caelestia,* oct. 591—Jaffé, n. 1159.

[12] C. 4, D. XLVII—*Nec novum nec,* iul. 600—Jaffé, n. 1788.

[13] C. 16, X, *de regularibus et transeuntibus ad religionem,* III, 31—*Ad apostolicam sedem,* 23 nov. 1198—Potthast, n. 434.

[14] Bernardus Parmensis († 1266), *Glossa Ordinaria,* ad c. 16, X, *de regularibus et transeuntibus ad religionem,* III, 31, v. *Anni.*

[15] Hostiensis, Cardinalis (Henricus de Segusio), *Commentaria in Quinque Decretalium Libros* (5 vols. in 3, Venetiis, 1581), tit. *de temporibus ordinationum et qualitate ordinandorum,* c. *Dilectus filius* (I, 11, 15).

observed. In fact, the provincial councils of Fritzlar (1246),[16] Mainz (1261),[17] Exeter (1287)[18] and Béziers (1310)[19] find it necessary to stress the need for commendatory testimonials.

Ioannes Andreae concurs in this opinion by declaring "that those presented by other bishops ought to be examined by the one authorized to ordain."[20] However, he also points out that the obligation primarily rests with the proper bishop since he must make provision for the candidate.

The law itself is clear enough in stating that a bishop is not to ordain the subjects of another without the proper testimonials *(commendatitiae)*.[21] The presentation of these testimonials relieves the ordaining bishop of whatever obligation he might have in the matter, excepting the case in which a known criminal is presented for ordination.[22] It is precisely because he knows of the qualifications of a man that commendatory letters are given by the proper bishop.[23] The bishop receiving the testimonials may put such faith in them as to proceed to confer orders on their authority and without additional examination.[24]

Article II. *Examiners*

"It is regularly and generally observed that the right to examine belongs to him whose right it is to impose hands."[25] This principle, enunciated by Innocent III (1198-1216), is the epitome of leg-

---

[16] C. X, *De clericis peregrinis*—Mansi, XXIII, 728.

[17] C. XXXII, *De qualitate ordinandorum*—Mansi, XXIII, 1091.

[18] C. VIII, *De ordine in genere*—Mansi, XXIV, 797.

[19] C. VII—Mansi, XXV, 361.

[20] Novella, tit. *de praebendis et dignitatibus*, c. *Cum secundum* (III, 5, 16).

[21] C. 7, C. IX, q. 2—Council of Antioch (341), cap. XIII—Mansi, II, 1314.

[22] Cf. Ioannes Andreae, *Novella, loc. cit.*

[23] C. 2, C. XIX, q. 2—Urbanus II (1088-1099), *Urbanus Papa*—Jaffé, n. 5760.

[24] *Glossa*, ad. c. 8, C. XVI, q. 5, v. *Ordinet*. Cf. c. 37, C. VII, q. 1—IV Council of Carthage (398), cap. XXII—Mansi, III, 953; c. 33, C. XVI, q. 1—Council of Agde (506), cap. XXVII—Mansi, VIII, 329; c. 5, X, *de officio et potestate iudicis delegati*, I, 29—Alexander III (1159-1181), *Coniugatus*—Jaffé, n. 14104.

[25] C. 34, X, *de electione et electi potestate, I, 6—Innocentius III, Venerabilem fratrem nostrum*, mart. 1202—Potthast, n. 1653.

islation governing the examiner. From the canons treating of examinations prior to the reception of orders it is clear that the episcopal right to ordain has a corollary in the right to examine. For another to do this without a mandate is an infringement on this right and, consequently, illicit.[26] In fact, this right is of such a nature that the bishop may re-examine when another, authorized by the bishop, has already examined.[27]

The *Decretum Gratiani* does not specify that the duty of examining is entrusted to a particular official, although it does say that the archdeacon has charge of the preparation for ordinations.[28] There is expression only of the selection by the bishop of "priests and other prudent men, learned in the divine law and well versed in ecclesiastical ordinances"[29] to test the candidates. Obviously, the bishop may not haphazardly commission others to examine and thus relieve himself of an unwelcome obligation. As the ruler of the diocese, he has a serious responsibility in choosing examiners who meet the requirements of the law.[30] Through them the bishop himself is said to examine.[31] Consequently, in selecting he does not appoint men who are unsuitable, easily corrupted, or intellectually unfit. On the contrary, the bishop makes certain that the examiners are men who cannot be lured from their duty by the promise of favor or the desire of recompense for the approval of the unqualified.[32]

In his treatise St. Raymond omits consideration of the arch-

[26] Cf. Hostiensis, *Summa Aurea* (Venetiis, 1570), tit. *de temporibus ordinationum et qualitate ordinandorum,* v. *Et a quo* (I, 46 r).

[27] Hostiensis, Commentaria, tit. *de aetate et qualitate praeficiendorum,* c. Accepimus (I, 14, 13); *idem, Summa Aurea,* tit. *de scrutinio in ordine faciendo,* v. Quando fieri debet (I, 52 v).

[28] C. 1, D. XXV. Friedberg indicates that this canon is derived from Pseudo-Isidore.

[29] C. 5, D. XXIV—Council of Nantes, cap. XI—Mansi, XVIII a, 169.

[30] Cf. c. 3, C. X, q. 1—Leo IV (847-855), *Quanto studio,* anno 849—Jaffé, n. 2599; c. 5, C. X, q. 1—Council of Antioch (341), c. XXIV—Mansi, II, 1335.

[31] Cf. Rufinus, *Summa,* D. XXIV.

[32] C. 5, D. XXIV: Ipsi autem, quibus cura committitur, cavere debent, ne aut favoris gratia, aut cuiuscumque muneris cupiditate illecti a vero devient, ut indignum et minus idoneum ad sacros gradus suscipiendos episcopi manibus applicent.—Council of Nantes, cap. XI—Mansi, XVIII a, 169.

deacon's rôle in this regard because of the ambiguity surrounding this office. He notes that there are as many varieties of customs, concerning the duties and powers of this and some other offices, as there are churches.[33] This may be true as a general statement, but it has to be qualified in the present consideration.

Prior to the composition of the *Decretales Gregorii IX* there is reference to the right of the archdeacon as an examiner in a letter of Honorius III (1216-1227)[34] contained in the fifth of the *Compilationes Antiquae*. This missive is not incorporated into his work by St. Raymond. Instead, he prefers one by Innocent III (1198-1216), written to the Archbishop of Milan and stressing the point that by common law certain functions such as the examination of *ordinandi* belong to the archdeacon rather than to the chancellor.[35] Probably this earlier letter is chosen because it is for more explicit in its reference to the traditional rôle of the archdeacon. Whatever the reason, there is in it a precise statement of the position of the archdeacon relative to ordination whereas in the *Decretum Gratiani* there is only a generalization. For an unexplained reason Gratian fails to mention the ancient laws of the Church indicating direction of the junior clergy by the archdeacon. The solitary reference he does give presents a very incomplete picture of this important office.[36]

This designation of the archdeacon as an examiner is not to be construed as being in any way derogatory to the right of the bishop. It is understood as exercised as an aid to the bishop, for the latter

[33] Raymundus de Pennafort, *Summa*, III, t. 27. Cf. c. 2, X, *de excessibus praelatorum et subditorum*, V, 31—Alexander III (1159-1181), *Ad haec quoniam* —Jaffé, n. 13806; c. 6, X, *de consuetudine*, I, 4—Innocentius III (1198-1216), *Cum olim venerabilis*, 4 febr. 1209—Potthast, n. 3645.

[34] *Quinque Compilationes Antiquae necnon Collectio Canonum Lipsiensis* (ed. Friedberg, Lipsiae, 1882), (I, 13), c. 2—*Quid ad archidiaconi*, 1218-1220—Potthast, n. 7724.

[35] C. 9, X, *de officio archidiaconi*, I, 23—*Ut nostrum prodeat*, 23 sept. 1198 —Potthast, n. 377. Cf. Hostiensis, *Summa Aurea*, tit. *de scrutinio in ordine faciendo*, v. *Quando fieri debet* (I, 52 v).

[36] Cf. *Dictionnaire de Droit Canonique* (Commencé sous la direction de A. Villien et E. Magnin; continué sous la direction de A. Amanieu et R. Naz, Fasc. 1-15, Paris—VI: Libraire Letouzey et Ane, 1924-1939), "Archidiacre," 951, 953, 959, 967-9, 971.

may examine if he wishes to do so. The correlation of duties is best explained by saying that if the archdeacon is present at the convocation prior to the ordinations, the bishop delegates him to examine; if the archdeacon is absent, the bishop chooses qualified men to perform this task. In both cases the bishop himself may examine if he so desires. He enjoys this prerogative as well as the right to re-examine and to reject those whom the archdeacon or the other examiners may approve.[37] Thus, even though he has the right to examine from the common law, the archdeacon exercises this right in subjection to the bishop.

Article III. *Matter for Examination*

A. *General Aspects*

Throughout the *Corpus Iuris* there is a constant note of warning that the unworthy and less suitable are not to be ordained.[38] This testifies to the solicitude exercised in the selection of those accepted for holy orders. It is precisely to guarantee the presence of the necessary qualities, and to exclude the deficient, that examinations are prescribed. There is a diligent inquiry commanded by the law and applied in view of the general principle *quanto res est maior, tanto maior est inquisitio facienda.*[39]

---

[37] Cf. Hostiensis, *Summa Aurea,* tit. *de scrutinio in ordine faciendo,* v. *Quando fieri debet* (I, 52 v); Ioannes Andreae, *Novella,* tit. *de officio archidiaconi,* c. *Ad haec* (I, 23, 7).

[38] Cf. c. 5, D. XXIV—Council of Nantes, cap. XI—Mansi, XVIII a, 169; c. 5, D. LXI—Leo I (440-461), *Cum de ordinationibus,* 10 aug. 446 (?)—Jaffé, n. 410; c. 25, D. L—S. Augustinus, *Epistola Bonifacio*—Migne, *Patrologiae Cursus Completus, Series Latina* (221 vols., Parisiis, 1858-1864), XXXIII, 812; c. 4, D. XXIII—Clemens I (88?-97?), *Urget nos fratres*—Jaffé, n. † 12 (spurious); c. 15, C. VIII, q. 1—Origen, *In Leviticum,* homil. VI—*MPG,* XII, 469; c. 6, X, *de aetate et qualitate et ordine praeficiendorum,* I, 14—Alexander III (1158-1181), *Quaeris a nobis*—Jaffé, n. 13785; c. 13, X, *de aetate et qualitate et ordine praeficiendorum,* I, 14—Innocentius III (1198-1216), *Accepimus te nostris* Potthast, n. 5036; c. 14, X, *de aetate et qualitate et ordine praeficiendorum,* I, 14—IV Lateran Council (1215), cap. XXVII—Mansi, XXII, 1015.

[39] *Glossa,* ad c. 5, D. LXI, v. *Quanto.* Cf. c. 2, D. XLII—S. Ioannes Chrysostomus, *In Epistolam ad Hebraeos,* cap. VII, homil. XII—*MPG,* LXIII, 96; c. 2, D. LIX—Zosimus (417-418), *Exigit dilectio,* 21 febr. 418—Jaffé, n.

This is exemplified by the admonitions that bishops are not to be elected who have not passed from the state of a disciple to that of a teacher;[40] that popular clamor or the desire to quell a public disturbance are not sufficient reason for forsaking the investigation prior to ordination and thus run the risk of ordaining the unworthy;[41] that personal considerations offer no excuse for deviation from the common law.[42]

This is a general but incomplete view of the law. A more precise delineation is offered by reference to the basic texts of St. Paul forming the keystone for this legislation.

> Oportet ergo episcopum irreprehensibilem esse, unius uxoris virum, sobrium, prudentem, ornatum, pudicum, hospitalem, doctorem, non vinolentum, non cupidum, sed suae domui bene praepositum, filios habentem subditos cum omni castitate . . . non neophytum, ne in superbiam elatus in judicium incidat diaboli.[43]

> Oportet enim episcopum sine crimine esse, sicut Dei dispensatorem: non superbum, non iracundum, non vinolentum, non percussorem, non turpis lucri cupidum, sed hospitalem, benignum, sobrium, justum, sanctum, continentem, amplectentem eum, qui secundum doctrinam est, fidelem sermonem,

339; c. 45, C. I, 1—Symmachus (498-514), *Prodit religiosae*—Jaffé, n. † 760; c. 4, C. I, q. 7—II Council of Nicaea (787)—Mansi, XII, 992; c. 2, C. VII, q. 2—Gelasius I (492-496), *Nuper Foropopiliensis*—Jaffé n. 729; c. 7, X, *de electione et electi potestate*, I, 6—III Lateran Council (1179), cap. III—Mansi, XXII, 218.

40 C. 4, D. LIX—Zosimus (417-418), *Exigit dilectio*, 21 febr. 418—Jaffé, n. 369.

41 C. 5, D. LXI—Leo I (440-461), *Cum de ordinationibus*, 10 aug. 446 (?) —Jaffé, n. 410. Cf. c. 2, D. LXII—Coelestinus I (422-432), *Nulli sacerdotum*, 21 iul. 429—Jaffé, n. 410. Cf. c. 2, D. LXII—Coelestinus I (422-432), *Nulli sacerdotum*, 21 iul. 429—Jaffé, n. 371.

42 C. 55, D. L—IV Council of Carthage (398), cap. LXVIII—Mansi, III, 956; c. 3, D. LIX—Gregorius I (590-604), *Caput nostrum*, iul. 599—Jaffé, n. 1747; c. 1, D. LXXVIII—Bonifacius I (418-422), *Si quis triginta*—Jaffé, n. † 356; *Glossa*, ad c. 5, D. LXI, v. *Persona*.

43 1 *Tim.* III, 2-6.

ut potens sit exhortari in doctrina sana et eos, qui contradicunt arguere.[44]

These two texts are the foundation for the law, but an analysis of them in this dissertation is deferred until the character of the ordinand is considered. It is sufficient here, following the procedure of Gratian, to refer to canon 5 of distinction XXIV. It is there that the subjects on which the candidates are to be interrogated are enumerated.

In testing the ordinands the examiners must inquire into their natal origin, life, origin, place where educated, learning and, above all, knowledge of the law of God, as well as their age and title. Of these items particular attention is given to the origin of the aspirant in order to ascertain whether (a) he is of legitimate birth;[45] (b) he is a member of the diocese;[46] (c) he has a good name.[47]

These are the titles under which the matter for the examination is presented, but in this particular canon the listing is not marked by clear and exclusive distinctions. Instead, it is more of a generalization with the result that later canons in the *Corpus Iuris* emphasize the necessity of enquiry into three phases of the candidate's qualifications, viz., his age, knowledge, and character. In conformity with this procedure, the same restriction is employed here.

B. *Specific Considerations*

1. *Age*

An investigation into the age of the candidate is clearly indicated as matter for the examination. In the case of a candidate for the priesthood it is considered a violation of the law of St. Paul[48] to impose hands before he attains maturity.[49] Ioannes Andreae ex-

[44] *Titus*, I, 7-9.

[45] C. 1, X, *de filiis presbyterorum ordinandis vel non*, I, 17—Council of Poitiers (1078), can. VIII—Mansi, XX, 498.

[46] C. 4, *de clericis peregrinis, I, 22*—Honorius III (1216-1227), *Te nobis proponente*, 1216-1225—Potthast, n. 7512b.

[47] C. 6, D. XXXIII—Innocentius I (401?-417), *Mirari non possumus*—Jaffé, n. 314.

[48] 1 *Tim*. V, 22.

[49] C. 3, D. LXXVIII—Leo I (440-461), *Cum de ordinationibus*, 10 aug. 446 (?)—Jaffé, n. 410.

pressly notes that such an ordination is illicit.[50]

The legislation of popes and councils guides the examiners by stating the ages observed in the reception of orders. The candidate may become a porter, lector and exorcist between his seventh and twelfth years of age.[51] After his twelfth year the candidate may ascend to the order of acolyte.

The first of the major orders may be received when the twenty-first year is attained.[52] After the twenty-fifth year the ordinand is eligible for the diaconate,[53] and after the thirtieth, the priesthood.[54]

As explained here, this is the common law as found in the *Decretum.* With the provisions of the Third Lateran Council (1179) there is one notable change. This is a relaxation permitting ordination to the priesthood on the attaining of twenty-five years.[55] Gregory IX (1227-1241) retains this provision with the result that it is found in the collection bearing his name.[56]

2. *Knowledge*

The principle governing the investigation into the knowledge of the prospective recipient of orders is succinctly expressed in the *Decretum: Ignorantia mater cunctorum errorum maxime in sacer-*

[50] *Novella,* tit. *de electione et electi potestate,* c. *Nihil est* (I, 6, 44).

[51] C. 2, D. LXXVII—Zosimus (417-418), *Exigit dilectio,* 21 febr. 418—Jaffé, n. 339; c. 3, D. LXXVII—Siricius (384-398), *Directa ad decessorem,* 10 febr. 385—Jaffé, n. 255; c. 4, *de temporibus ordinationum et qualitate ordinandorum,* I, 9 in VIo.

[52] C. 4, D. LXXVII—Council of Constantinople (692)—Mansi, XII, 47 (Concilium Pseudosextum Universale et Reprobatum).

[53] C. 5, D. LXXVII—III Council of Carthage (397), cap. IV—Mansi, III, 880; c. 6, D. LXXVII—Council of Agde (506), cap: XVI—Mansi, VIII, 327. Cf. c. 14, X, *de temporibus ordinationum et qualitate ordinandorum,* I, 11—Honorius III (1216-1227), *Vel non est,* 28 iul. 1217—Potthast, n. 7720.

[54] C. 6, D. LXXVII—*loc. cit.;* c. 1, D. LXXVIII—Bonifacius I (418-422), *Si quis triginta*—Jaffé, n. †356; c. 4, D. LXXVIII—Council of Neocaesarea (314), can. XI—Mansi, II 541,

[55] I *Comp., de electione et electi potestate* (I, 4), c. 16.

[56] C. 7, X, *de electione et electi potestate,* I, 6—III Lateran Council (1179), cap. III—Mansi, XXII, 218.

dotibus Dei vitanda est.[57] This is the foundation on which the remainder of this particular legislation may be said to rest. Because of it there is the prescription that the examiners ascertain of the candidate the place of his education and his learning, especially his knowledge of the law of God.[58] Ignorance in the priest is truly considered intolerable,[59] inexcusable and unpardonable.[60] Moreover, the latitude of this consideration is such as to embrace all orders, and not merely the priesthood, for what is said of one is pertinent to the others.[61]

This demand for knowledge is not to be construed in such a way as to require that all clerics be stars in the intellectual firmament. Certainly the illiterate are not to be ordained, but it is quite possible that one of little knowledge be approved if there is hope for his progress. If, on the other hand, there is no such hope, he is not allowed to receive orders unless some great and urgent necessity demands this. This is the opinion advanced by Ioannes Andreae,[62] but this author also admits the strength of an opposing contention, defended by *alii,* supported by various texts of the *Decretum,* and claiming that punishment is to be meted out to those approving the unworthy, even in the case of necessity.[63]

It is common teaching that competency, more than brilliance, is sought by the examiners.[64] The basic requirement is that the as-

[57] C 1, D. XXXVIII—IV Council of Taledo (633), cap. XXV—Mansi, X, 626.

[58] C. 5, D. XXIV—Council of Nantes, cap. XI—Mansi, III, 884.

[59] C. 2, D. XXXVIII—IV Council of Toledo (633), cap. XXV—Mansi, X, 627.

[60] C. 3, D. XXXVIII—Leo I (440-461), *Licet de his, quae,* 17 mart. 450—Jaffé, n. 447. Cf. *Glossa,* ad D. XXXVI, v. *Simplicitatis.*

[61] C. 6, C. XXIV, q. 1—S. Augustinus, *In Ioannis Evangelium,* tract. L, cap. XII—*MPL,* XXXV, 1763 Cf. *Glossa,* ad c. 1, D. XXXVIII, v. *Ad Timotheum;* ad c. 5, D. LXI, v. *Omnium.*

[62] *Novella,* tit. *de electione et electi potestate,* c. *Cum in cunctis* (I, 6, 7).

[63] Cf. c. 5, D. XXIV—Council of Nantes, cap. XI—Mansi, XVIII a, 169; D. XXXVIII.

[64] Cf. c. 19, X, *de electione et electi potestate,* I, 6—Innocentius III, *Cum olim nobis,* 21 febr. 1200—Potthast, n. 949; *Glossa,* ad c. 1, C. XXXVI, v. *Illiteratos;* S. Raymundus, *Summa,* III, t. 5; Hostiensis, *Summa Aurea,* tit.

pirants know what befits the various orders.[65] Beyond this natural necessity there are no specific norms. Consequently it is possible to do no more than point out the general rules on which the commentators are in agreement.[66]

In the first part of the *Decretum,* from the thirty-sixth to the fortieth distinctions, Gratian outlines a course to be followed in this investigation of the candidate. The ordinand must have knowledge of (a) *sacred scripture:* if this is lacking no one may presume to promote an aspirant to the clerical state,[67] for ignorance of the Scriptures is considered ignorance of Christ,[68] and it is essential that priests know the Scriptures and canons in order that they may be able to lead the people by their faith and example;[69] (b) *secular writings:* as an ancillary element conductive to piety and an understanding of the Sacred Scripture, and because of the aid they give in distinguishing between truth and falsehood, in knowing the law, in understandiing the prophets and for certifying belief in the gos-

de temporibus ordinationum et qualitate ordinandorum, v. *Quarta regula prudentem* (I, 48 v.); *ibid., de aetate et qualitate et ordine praeficiendorum,* v. *Scientia* (I, 56).

[65] Cf. c. 1, D. XXV for a listing of duties for all orders.

[66] Note: Although not included in their collections by Gratian and St. Raymond there are several other instances in which the proper authorities are admonished to exercise care in the examination of ordinands. Cf. Gregorius I (590-604), *Qualiter erga,* iul. 593—*Monumenta Germaniae Historica, Gregorii I Papae Registrum Epistolarum* (4 vols., ed. L.M. Hartmann post Pauli Ewaldi obitum, Berolini, 1887-1899), t. I, Pars II, Liber III, n. 48; Gregorius I, *Fratris et coepiscopi,* mai. 594—*op. cit.,* Liber IV, n. 26; *idem, Indicavit nobis,* mart. 596—*op. cit.,* Liber VI, n. 27; *Interrogationes Examinationes,* post a. 803—*MGH, Legum Sectio II: Capitularia Regum Francorum,* t. I (ed. A. Boretius, Hannoverae, 1883), n. 116.

[67] C. I, D. XXXVI—Gelasius I (492-496), *Ad Episcopos Lucaniae,* cap. XVI—*MPL,* LIX, 53.

[68] C. 9, D. XXXVIII—S. Hieronymus, *In Isaiam Prophetam,* Prologus, nn. 1-2—*MPL,* XXIV, 17.

[69] C. 3, D. XXXVI—Origen, *In Leviticum,* homil. VI—*MPG,* XII, 474; c. 1, D. XXXVIII—IV Council of Toledo (633), cap XXV—Mansi, X, 626; c. 4, D. XXXVIII—Leo I (440-461), *Licet de his, quae,* 22 febr. 450—Jaffé, n. 447.

pel, grammar and dialectic are fostered;[70] (c) *secular business:* the ordinand also ought to have knowledge of secular affairs, since he is to administer not only to the spiritual but also to the temporal necessities of his subjects.[71]

3. *Character*

The third aspect of the candidate requiring examination is his character. It is of small import that a subject meets all the exactions of age and knowledge if he is so deficient in character as to be considered unworthy of ordination. With the two requisites already treated, this final consideration forms a trinity of necessary matter when an examination is required.

In the *Decretum Gratiani* the two texts of St. Paul,[72] enumerating the marks characteristic of the clerical state, determine the basis for investigation. However, these extracts follow the wording of the Apostle only in a general manner so as to serve as a framework for the treatment by Gratian.

In his selective combination of these two texts Gratian indicates that *crimen* does not include every sin; rather he calls *criminale peccatum* or *criminalis infamia* those sins, mortal and venial, proceeding from a deliberate will and committed after the reception of baptism.[73] The most important of these are listed as *sacrilegium, homicidium, adulterium, fornicatio,*[74] *falsum testimonium,*[75] *rapina,*

[70] C. 14, D. XXXVII—S. Clemens, *Epistola Fratribus Julio et Juliano—MPL,* CXXX, 58 (pseudo-Isidore); C. 8, D. XXXVII—Ven. Beda, *In Samuelem Prophetam,* lib. II, cap. IX—*MPL,* XCI, 589; c. 9, D. XXXVII—S. Ambrosius, *Expositio Evangelii secundum Lucam,* lib. 1, cap. 2—*MPL,* XV, 1533; c. 10, D. XXXVII—S. Hieronymus, *In Epistolam ad Titum,* cap. I—*MPL,* XXVI, 558.

[71] C. un., D. XXXIX—Gregorius I (590-604), *Nec novum nec*—Jaffé, n. 1788.

[72] 1 *Tim.,* III, 2-6; *Titus,* I, 7-9.

[73] D. XXV, III Pars.

[74] Cf. c. 1, D. LXXXI—S. Augustinus, *In Ioannis Evangelium,* tract. XLI, cap. VIII—*MPL,* XXXV, 1697; c. 5, D. L—Nicolaus I (858-867), *Sciscitaris itaque,* 861 (?), Jaffé, n. 2688; c. 29, D. L—Hormisdas (514-523), *Ecce mani-*

furtum,[76] *superbia, invidia, avaritia, iracundia, ebrietas.*

Whereas Gratian is satisfied with an enumeration of these crimes and a deferment of a more complete treatment to the fiftieth distinction, he exercises greater care in the case of the other attributes demanded by St. Paul. There is a relatively lengthly consideration of the continence required in orders, and it is indicated that a bishop is to be the husband of one wife; priests and deacons who have or wish wives may not be advanced in orders; no one is to receive the subdiaconate without a promise of chastity.[77]

Gratian further shows that the candidate is not to be given to the drinking of wine but is to be conservative in food and drink;[78] he is to be prudent;[79] he should be an honor to his state both in the exercise of virtue and in general appearance,[80] should receive the poor,[81] be discreet in his silence and speech,[82] should not be so irascible as to harm another either spiritually or physically.[83] The ordinand should not be so proud as to be unable to teach humbly;[84] he is not to be a usurer lest he sin against justice,[85] nor is he to be a recent convert.[86] Finally, in the two canons of distinction XLIX there is a compendious treatment of the vices from which the candidate should be free. For an unexplained reason Gratian defers treatment of the requisite ability of the ordinand as a ruler to a much later chapter.[87]

festissme—Jaffé, n. † 868; c. 13, D. LXXXI. The last canon listed is of uncertain origin, but one similar to it is found in the Council of Neocaesarea (314-325)—Mansi, II, 540.

[75] C. 7, D. L.—Council of Pamiers (517), can. XXII—Mansi, VIII, 561.

[76] C. 1, D. LXXXI—S. Augustinus, *In Ioannis Evangelium,* tract. XLI, cap. VIII—*MPL,* XXXV, 1697.

[77] D. XXVI—D. XXXIV.

[78] DD. XXXV, XLIV: . . . sobrium . . . non vinolentum.

[79] DD. XXXVI—XXXIX: . . . prudentem.

[80] DD. XL—XLI: . . . ornatum.

[81] DD. XLII, LXXXV: . . . hospitalem.

[82] D. XLV: . . . non percussorem.

[83] D. XLIII: . . . pudicum.

[84] D. XLVI: . . . non litigiosum.

[85] D. XLVII: . . . non cupidum.

[86] D. XLVIII: . . . non neophytum..

[87] D. LXXXIX: . . . suae domui bene praepositum.

Article IV. *Complementary Aspects*

A. *Sanctions*

In the distinction setting forth the general legislation on examinations prior to the reception of orders there is this statement:

> Si quis presbiter aut diaconus sine aliqua examinatione ordinati sunt, aut certe, cum discuterentur, criminosa peccata sua confessi sunt, aut post ordinationem ab aliis detecti, abiciantur ex clero. § 1. Similiter vero et de universo clericorum ordine servetur; nam hoc sibi, quod irreprehensibile est, sancta ecclesia catholica defendit.[88]

From the text it is clear that the old law envisions not only the case of ordination without an examination, but also includes the sanction applicable when a crime is confessed in the process of the examination. Moreover there is a penalty for a crime concealed at the time of ordination but discovered afterwards.[89]

What is here set forth regarding the necessity of the examination is understood in the light of the distinctions made in the first article of this chapter. It can hardly be said that the omission of the examination is in itself a cause for deposition if the recipient is suitable in other respects. There has to be a further qualifying condition. In such a case it seems that the ordaining minister is culpable rather than the ordinand, since the necessity of deciding whether or not the candidate is to be examined ultimately devolves on the bishop or his agent.[90]

If the candidate admits during the examination that he is guilty of a serious crime *(crimina manifesta)*, this is sufficient cause for rejection. If such a crime is concealed, detection after ordination results in deposition from the clerical state.[91] Crime is here understood

[88] C. 7, D. XXIV—I Council of Nicaea (325), can. IX— Mansi, II, 671.

[89] Cf. c. 4, D. LXXXI—I Council of Nicaea, can. IX— *loc. cit.*

[90] Cf. c. 1, D. LXX—Council of Chalcedon (451), can. VI—Mansi, VII, 375; c. 32, C. XVI, q. 7—IX Council of Toledo (655), cap. II—Mansi, XI, 26.

[91] C. 5, D. XXIV—Council of Nantes, cap. XI—Mansi, XVIII a, 169; c. 55, D. L—IV Council of Carthage (398), cap. LXVIII: Ex penitentibus, quamvis sit bonus, tamen clericus non ordinetur. Si per ignorantiam episcopi factum fuerit, deponatur a clero, quia se ordinationis tempore non prodidit

in the restricted sense of a major offense requiring public penance. In the event that the one ordained is guilty of a minor crime, this is a matter for penance but not for deposition.[92] Later Gregory IX (1227-1234) admits this same distinction of major and minor crimes when asked about adultery, perjury, homicide and false testimony in priests.[93]

Judging from the legislation on this matter, it may be said that the ordinand guilty of a major crime is obliged to make this fact known.[94] When questioned during the examination, he is to confess his guilt that, as Hostiensis[95] notes, a dispensation may be granted for an impediment to the reception of orders. This same author[96] does not hesitate to declare that if an unworthy candidate is ordained, the presumption is against the one ordaining. Ignorance concerning a defect in one's own subject cannot easily be alleged. It is because of this assumption that a sentence against a cleric is prejudicial to the one who ordained him.[97]

St. Leo I (440-461) points out that if the bishop ordains without examining, the minister in this case violates the law of St. Paul

fuisse penitentem—Mansi, III, 956; c. 5, D. LXXXI—I Council of Nicaea (325), can. X: Quicumque ex his, qui lapsi sunt, per ignorantiam iam ordinati sunt, vel contemptu eorum, qui eos ordinaverunt, hoc non preiudicat regulae ecclesiasticae. Cum enim compertum fuerit, deponentur.—Mansi, II, 671.

[92] C. 1, D. LXVIII—Gregorius I (590-604), *Quod multis scriptis,* iul. 592: Sed si quis cum levi culpa ad sacerdotium venit, pro culpa penitencia debet indici, et tamen ordo servetur.—Jaffé, n. 1198. For examples of minor crimes cf. c. 17, D. XVIII—XVI Council of Toledo (693), cap. VII—Mansi, XII, 74; c. 13, C. I, q. 4—*Codex Iustinianus* (recensivit Paulus Krueger, Berolini, 1877, (8.4) 7; c. 3, C. V, q. 4—XI Council of Toledo (675), cap. I—Mansi, XI, 137.

[93] C. 17, X, *de temporibus ordinationum et qualitate ordinandorum,* I, 11—*Quaesitum est de,* 21 mart. 1227—4 sept. 1234—Potthast, n. 9550.

[94] C. 7, D. XXIV—I Council of Nicaea (325), can. IX—Mansi, II, 671; c. 3, D. LXXXI—Coelestinus I (422-432), *Cuperemus quidem,* 22 iul. 428—Jaffé, n. 369.

[95] *Summa Aurea,* tit. *de scrutinio in ordiine faciendo,* v. *Quid si promovendus in scrutinio* (I, 53 v.).

[96] Hostiensis, *Commentaria,* tit. *de aetate et qualitate et ordine praeficiendorum,* c. *Cum sit ars* (I, 14, 14).

[97] C. D. LXXXI Coelestinus I (422-432), *Cuperemus quidem,* 26 iul. 428—Jaffé, n. 369; c. 4, D. LIX—*loc. cit.;* c. 10, C. III, q. 6—Nicolaus I (858-867), *Proposuerat quidem,* 26 maii 865—Jaffé, n. 2789.

and, as the Apostle indicates, shares in the sin of another.[98]

On the other hand, the bishop also may be blameworthy when he does examine. If he is negligent in failing to examine diligently, the bishop is responsible and there are penalties to which he is liable.[99] Thus, should he ordain a boy of thirteen to the diaconate, he is suspended so as to be unable to confer orders, while the recipient is suspended from the exercise of the diaconate until the required age is attained.[100]

Even when he examines through others the bishop must safeguard his own position by selecting examiners who are commonly though to be qualified. If this is done, the bishop is exonerated should the unworthy be presented for ordination. In this case the men commissioned to examine or the archdeacon, if he acts *ex officio,* are punished.[101]

Should the bishop act maliciously in selecting the examiners in that he chooses men unsuited for the position, he can hardly be excused. In fact, Hostiensis[102] declares that the choice of such examiners is usually due to the recognized defects of the candidate and the desire of the bishop to excuse himself by entrusting the examination to those incapable of handling it.

[98] C. 3, D. LXXVIII—*Cum de ordinationibus,* 10 aug. 446 (?)—Jaffé, n. 410.

[99] Cf. Hostiensis, *Commentaria,* tit. *de aetate et qualitate et ordine praeficiendorum,* c. *Accepimus* (I, 14, 13).

[100] C. 14, X, *de temporibus ordinationum et qualitate ordinandorum,* I, 11 —Honorius III (1216-1227), *Vel non est,* 28 iul. 1217—Potthast, n. 7720. For penalties when the bishop is guilty of a delict in ordaining, cf. c. 2, D. XXXVI —Zosimus (417-418), *Exigit dilectio,* 21 febr. 418—Jaffé, n. 339; c. 1, D. LI—Innocentius I (401?-417), *Saepe me et,* c. 404—Jaffé, n. 292; c. 2, D. LV—IV Council of Arles (524), can. I—Mansi, VIII, 626; c. 8, D. LXIV—I Council of Nicaea (325), can. VI—Mansi, II, 671; c. 8, C. I, q. 1—Council of Chalcedon (451), can. II—Mansi, VII, 373; c. 13, X, *de temporibus ordinationum et qualitate ordinandorum,* I, 11—Innocentius III (1198-1216), *Litteras vestras recepimus,* mart.—apr. 1201—Potthast, n. 1327; c. 15, *h.t.*—Innocentius III, *Dilectus filius* W., 5 ian. 1211—Potthast, n. 4163.

[101] Cf. Hostiensis, *op. cit.;* Ioannes Andreae, *Novella,* tit. *de aetate et qualitate et ordine praeficiendorum,* c. *Accepimus* (I, 14, 13); *Glossa,* ad c. 14, X, *de aetate et qualitate et ordine praeficiendorum,* I, 14, v. *Deprehendi.*

[102] *Commentaria,* tit. *de electione et electi potestate,* c. *Nihil est* (I, 6, 44).

B. *Time, Place, Form*

These final considerations are presented here, not because of any subordination in importance, but due to a dearth of source material concerning them.

No more can be said than that two examinations are involved in the reception of orders. The first of these commences on Wednesday *(feria quartâ)* and continues for the three days preceding the Saturday on which orders are conferred.[103]

In the older law there is evidence that the candidates go to the city of the episcopal residence in order to be examined.[104] In later legislation the procedure is reversed and the commentators speak of the coming of the bishop both to conduct the examination and to ordain.[105] The *Glossa Ordinaria*[106] indicates that the title *"De scrutinio in ordine faciendo"* is the decretal counterpart of the legislation found in *Decretum Gratiani.* It seems, though, that a distinction should be made inasmuch as the *Decretum* emphasizes the three days of examination prior to the conferring of orders whereas the title in the *Decretales Gregorii IX* refers to an interrogation that is a part of the actual ceremony of ordination. Certainly, Hostiensis[107] makes the distinction, for he expressly speaks of a second examination *ante altare* on Saturday.[108] Ioannes Andreae is in complete accord with this for he also distinguishes a twofold *scrutinium:* (1) *quod habetur ante ordinationem;* (2) *quod fit in ordinatione.*[109]

[103] C. 5, D. XXIV—Council of Nantes, cap. XI—Mansi, XVIII a, 169.

[104] *Loc. cit.;* Rufinus, *Summa Decretorum,* D. XXIV.

[105] Cf. Hostiensis, *Summa Aurea,* tit. *de scrutinio in ordine faciendo,* v. *Quando fieri debet* (I, 52 v.).

[106] Ad c. un., X, *de scrutinio in ordine faciendo,* I, 12.

[107] *Loc. cit.:* Patet ex praemisis quando fieri debet primum scrutinium, quia feria quarta ante sabbatum, in quo ordines celebrantur; secundum vero in ipsa ordinatione.

[108] Hostiensis, *Summa Aurea,* tit. *de scrutinio in ordine faciendo,* v. *Quando fieri debet* (I, 52 v.): Forma vero secundi scrutinii haec est, quia in Romana ecclesia prior diaconorum, in ecclesiis aliis major diaconus, id est Archidiaconus dicit ante altare: 'postulat sancta mater ecclesia hunc subdiaconum, vel diaconum ad onus diaconatus, vel presbyteratus assumi,' et ordinario interrogante, 'scis eum esse dignum,' respondet. . . . .

[109] *Novella,* tit, *de scrutinio in ordine faciendo,* (I, 12).

CHAPTER II

TRIDENTINE AND POST-TRIDENTINE LAW

Article I. *Nexus between Decretal and Tridentine Law*

The observation of Hostiensis († 1271)[1] regarding a general failure to observe the laws governing the *scrutinia* prior to ordination finds confirmation as late as two hundred and fifty years after the time of his writing. The gap between the Decretals and the Tridentine legislation is bridged by little in the way either of emphasis on existing law or of new decrees. This paucity of new enactments does not point to so close an adherence to the law as to make additional legislation unnecessary. On the contrary, it is indicative of imperfect observance. The decrees of the *Corpus Iuris* are sufficient, but obedience to them during this period is marked by laxity. Due to both the unfortunate circumstances of the times and also the lack of care on the part of bishops, desuetude is the outstanding characteristic of this institute.[2]

Despite the existence of abuses, Leo X (1513-1517) in the Constitution *Dum intra*[3] of the Fifth Lateran Council (1512-1517) does no more than attempt a clarification of the relationship between various superiors. The only result of this is the prescription whereby religious desirous of promotion to orders are examined through the ordinary and, if found qualified, are admitted to ordination. Legislation so limited in scope could hardly cope with evils so widespread.

In the Provincial Council of Sens (1528)[4] there is a more

[1] *Commentaria,* tit. *de temporibus ordinationum et qualitate ordinandorum,* c. *Dilectus filius* (I, 11, 15).

[2] Benedictus XIV, *De Synodo Dioecesana* (2 vols. in 1, Neapoli, 1772), V, cap. 2, n. 3; Wernz, *Ius Decretalium* (6 vols., Romae et Prati, 1898-1905), II, n. 68.

[3] *Codicis Iuris Canonici Fontes* (cura Emi Petri Card. Gasparri editi, 9 vols., Romae [postea Civitate Vaticana]: Typis Polyglottis Vaticanis, 1923-1939. Vols. VII-IX ed. cura et studio Emi Iustiniani Card. Serédi), n. 72, § 11.

[4] Decreta III-VII—Mansi, XXXII, 1185.

thorough attempt at reform. The decrees of this council require that the testimonials of the parish priest bear witness to the proper age and faultless life of the ordinand. On the satisfaction of these two requirements, there is an investigation of his learning. His knowledge should include, as far as is humanly possible, the books enumerated in c. 5, D. XXXVIII, of the *Decretum Gratiani*.[5]. It is only after this examination that dimissorial letters are granted.

In this same council there are several indications of the existence of abuses. One of these is the demand for a diligent investigation of clerics already promoted to the priesthood. Those ordained before the proper age are to be suspended; those whose life is reprehensible are to be subjected to coercive measures; those lacking sufficient knowledge are to be suspended from the exercise of orders until they become versed in the learning required by their status.

A second corrective measure is occasioned by the practice whereby those who are aware of their ignorance, their lack of ability, or their crime, seek to be ordained at the Roman curia. They do this to avoid being examined by their own bishop. Since these men leave without dimissorials and since their ordination is of doubtful sanction, on returning to their proper diocese they are not to be allowed to exercise orders until there is a diligent perusal of their letters, an investigation into the power and authorization of the ordaining prelate, and an examination into the life, knowledge, age and patrimony of the one claiming ordination. Deficiency in any respect suffices for suspension.

Unfortunately this lack of observance of the law in the matter of examining ordinands is so widespread that in 1538 a gathering of cardinals and other prelates, in reporting to Paul III (1534-1549), stigmatizes the condition as the first and gravest abuse to be corrected in a reform of the Church. Because it is the immediate forerunner of the Tridentine legislation, the pertinent paragraph of the report is here quoted in full:

> Primus abusus in hac parte est ordinatio clericorum, &

[5] *Capitulare Ahytonis Episcopi Basiliensis*, n. VI: . . . ipsis sacerdotibus necessaria ad discendum, id est sacramentorum liber, lectionarius, antiphonarius, baptisterium, computus, canones penitentiales, psalterium, omeliae per circulum anni dominicis diebus et singulis festivitatibus aptae.—Mansi, XIV, 395.

praesertim presbyterorum, in qua nulla adhibetur cura, nulla adhibetur diligentia: quod passim quicumque sint, imperitissimi sint, villissimo genere orti, sint malis moribus ornati, sint adolescentes, admittantur ad ordines sacros, & maxime ad presbyteratum, ad characterem, inquam, Christum maxime exprimentem. Hinc innumera scandala, hinc contemptus ordinis ecclesiastici, hinc divini cultus veneratio non tantum diminuta, sed etiam prope jam extincta. Ideo putamus optimum fore, si sanctitas vestra primo in hac urbe praeficeret huic negotio duos aut tres praelatos, viros doctos et probos, qui ordinationibus clericorum praeessent. Injungeret etiam episcopis omnibus, adhibitis etiam poenis censurarum, ut id curarent in suis dioecesibus. Nec permittat sanctitas vestra ut quispiam ordinetur, nisi ab episcopo suo, vel cum licentia deputatorum in urbe, aut episcopi sui: insuper ut in Ecclesiis suis quisque episcopus magistrum habeat, a quo clerici minores & litteris & moribus instruantur, ut iura praecipiunt.[6]

It is against this background that the laws of the Council of Trent on the sacrament of orders are viewed. In considering this council and subsequent legislation prior to the Code, the division of material suggested in the Council of Trent[7] and accepted as classic by the commentators[8] is followed. This consists of (1) the preliminary investigation of the candidate, and (2) the examination into his origin, age, character, knowledge and title on the Wednes-

[6] Consilium Delectorum Cardinalium & Aliorum Praelatorum de Emendanda Ecclesia—Mansi, XXXV A, 349.

[7] Sess. XXIII, *de ref.*, cc. 5, 7.

[8] Cf. Engel (1634-1674), *Collegium Universi Iuris Canonici* (ed. 10, Salisburgi, 1726), lib. I, tit. 12, c. un.; Reiffenstuel (1641-1703), *Jus Canonicum Universum* (5 vols. in 7, Parisiis, 1864-1870), lib. I, tit. 12, n. 2; Gonzalez-Tellez († ca. 1674), *Commentaria Perpetua in Singulos Texus Quinque Librorum Decretalium Gregorii IX* (5 vols., Venetiis, 1699), lib. I, tit. 12; Schmalzgrueber (1663-1735), *Jus Ecclesiasticum Universum* (5 vols. in 12, Romae, 1843-1845), lib. I, tit. 12, n. 1; Devoti (1744-1820), *Institutionum Canonicarum Libri IV* (4 vols., Romae, 1815), lib. I, tit. 4, sect. II; De Angelis (1824-1881), *Praelectiones Iuris Canonici* (5 vols., Romae, 1908), lib. I, tit. 12; Wernz (1842-1914), *Ius Decretalium,* II, n. 40; Gasparri (1852-1934), *De Sacra Ordinatione* (2 vols., Parisiis, 1893-1894), n. 674.

day before the ordination. These two examinations are the Tridentine counterpart of the *scrutinium ante ordinationem* of decretal law.

Article II. *Preliminary Examination of the Candidate*

A. *Council of Trent to the Constitution* Speculatores

1. *General Necessity*

In the twenty-third session, on reformation, of the Council of Trent (1545-1563) there is an effective restatement of the care of the Church concerning the status of those who receive orders. This solicitude is given general expression in the third chapter of this session, where it is stated that a bishop, when prevented by illness from ordaining his own subjects, is to examine and approve these ordinands before sending them to another bishop for ordination.[9] Barbosa (1589-1649)[10] explains this prescription in the light of the seventh session, on reformation, the eleventh chapter. Prior to granting dimissorial letters the bishop examines the candidate to ascertain his capacity for orders. Besides testifying concerning the result of this inquiry, the reason which prevents the proper bishop from ordaining is also expressed in writing.[11] It seems that any just cause, and not only poor health, is sufficient to permit this procedure.[12]

Shortly after the conclusion of the Tridentine Council a deviation from this course is permitted. A reply of the Sacred Congregation of the Council indicates that it is permissible for the bishop (a) after examining, to grant dimissorial letters, or (b) to leave the examination to the one who ordains.[13] A year later another reply again stresses the point that when dimissorials are granted, it is licit to commission the ordaining prelate to examine.[14]

[9] Conc. Trident., sess. XXIII, *de ref.*, c. 3. Use is made of the text and translation of the text of the Council by Schroeder (1875-1942), *Canons and Decrees of the Council of Trent* (St. Louis: Herder, 1941).

[10] *Collectanea Doctorum in Varia Concilii Tridentini Decreta et Canones* (Lugduni, 1657), ad sess. XXIII, c. 3.

[11] Conc. Trident., sess. VII, *de ref.*, c. 11.

[12] Cf. III Provincial Council of Milan (1573), c. X—Mansi, XXXIV A, 152.

[13] *Ventimilien.*, mense dec. 1587, ad 14—*Fontes*, n. 2194.

[14] S.C.Ep. et Reg., *Caietana*, 20 dec. 1588—*Fontes*, n. 1420.

Some freedom of action is also conceded to the ordaining bishop. When a candidate presents his letters which contain the assertion that he has been examined and found qualified, the bishop may accept these testimonials; but he is not obliged to do so.[15] If he wishes, he himself may examine the aspirant.[16] If the bishop either knows or finds the ordinand to be unworthy he sins in ordaining him.[17] Under ordinary circumstances the ordaining prelate is assured by the testimonials he receives, for the proper bishop has the fundamental responsibility of insuring the fitness of the candidate, and it is presumed that he examines the candidate to establish this status.[18]

2. *Particular Requisites*

The above principles are those recognized as the common law. With the notable exception of the Fifth Provincial Council of Milan (1579),[19] the particular legislation of such councils as those of Ravenna (1568),[20] Malines (1570),[21] Genoa (1574),[22] Bordeaux (1583)[23] Sorrento (1584),[24] Cambrai (1586),[25] Avignon (1594),[26] Aquileia (1596),[27] Sienna (1599)[28] and, again, Cambrai (1631),[29] conforms to the general law.

Tonsure is not conferred on those who have not received the

[15] S.C.C., *Mileten.*, 20 nov. 1592—*Fontes*, n. 2252.

[16] S.C.C., *Nullius*, 16 ian. 1593—*Fontes*, n. 2253; 17 ian. 1693—*Fontes*, n. 2934.

[17] Cf. Fagnanus (1598-1678), *Commentaria in Libros Decretalium* (5 vols. in 3, Coloniae Allobrogum, 1759), ad c. 11, X, *de praebendis et dignitatibus*, III, n. 59.

[18] *Ibid.*, n. 56.

[19] Mansi, XXXIV A, 434.

[20] Tit. *de ordine*—Mansi, XXXV A, 622.

[21] *Decretum de ordinandis*—Mansi, XXXIV A, 582.

[22] C. XII, *De sacramento ordinis*—Mansi, XXXVI bis, 576.

[23] Tit. XIV—Mansi, XXXIV A, 759.

[24] Tit. XXVI, *De sacramento ordinis*—Mansi, XXXVI bis, 295.

[25] C. X—Mansi, XXXIV B, 1238.

[26] Tit. XIX—Mansi, XXXIV B, 1341.

[27] C. XI—Mansi, XXXIV B, 1400.

[28] C. XV, *De sacramento ordinis*—Mansi, XXXVI bis, 536.

[29] Tit. XII—Mansi, XXXVI ter, 178.

sacrament of confirmation or are entering the clerical state not in order to give faithful service to God but to flee a secular judgment.[30] In addition to this the Council of Rouen (1581)[31] requires a certificate from the pastor testifying that the candidate is the offspring of a legimate marriage.

For the minor orders a good testimonial is needed from the pastor of the candidate as well as from the master of the school where he is being educated.[32] According to Hallier (1595-1659),[33] the prefects of the seminary are included in this latter category.

The Council of Trent does not precisely specify what the contents of these testimonials are, but in chapter eleven of the same twenty-third session, on reformation, there is expressed the necessity of the ordinand's exercising, in the church to which he is assigned, the orders already received. Absence because of study is a legitimate reason for deviation from this rule. It is also expected that the advancement in orders is accompanied by an increase in worthiness of life and doctrine as demonstrated by good character, faithful service in the church, greater reverence toward priests and the higher orders, and more frequent communion.[34]

It is noteworthy that regulars are not included under the provisions of the fifth chapter of the twenty-third session, on reformation. The testimonials in which the regular superiors attest that the candidate for orders lacks none of the requisites are acceptable.[35]

[30] Conc. Trident., sess. XXIII, *de ref.*, c. 4.

[31] C. *de episcoporum officiis*, n. 4—Mansi, XXXIV A, 632.

[32] Conc. Trident., sess. XXIII, *re ref.*, c. 5.

[33] *De Sacris Electionibus et Ordinationibus ex Antiquo et Novo Ecclesiae Usu* (in Migne, *Theologiae Cursus Completus,* vol. XXIV, Parisiis, 1860), Pars. I, Sect. I, Cap. II, art. 3, n. 5.

[34] Conc. Trident., sess. XXIII, *de ref.*, c. 11. Cf. Provincial Council of Besançon (1571), tit. *de examine ordinandorum*, n. 5—Mansi, XXXVI bis, 62; Provincial Council of Avignon (1594), c. XIX—Mansi, XXXIV B, 1341. For the particular legislation governing Rome, cf. Alexander VII (1655-1667), *Apostolica sollicitudo,* 7 aug. 1662—*Fontes,* n. 239.

[35] S.C.C., *Mediolanen.*, mense aug. 1587, ad 4—*Fontes,* n. 2185; *Mileten.*, 27 apr. 1595—*Fontes,* n. 2285; *Monopolitana,* 27 febr. 1602—*Fontes,* n. 2345; *Regularium,* 28 febr. 1602—*Fontes,* n. 2346. Cf. Barbosa, *Collectanea,* sess. XXIII, c. 5; Fermosini († 1672), *Opera Omnia Canonica, Civilia, et Criminalia*

Those raised to any of the major orders go to the bishop a month before the ordination. Then this prelate, who by right controls the investigation into the life and character of the candidate, commissions the pastor or another, if this is preferable,[36] to announce publicly in the church the names and desires of those wishing to receive ordination.

The Council of Trent does not specify the day, how often and in what manner the publication is made. However, in the observance of the common law, the Provincial Council of Rouen (1581)[37] indicates that the bishop enlists the services of the rural dean to inform the pastor, or other priest commissioned to investigate, of the impending ordination. They then see to it that the name and intention of the candidate is publicly announced in the church on three Sundays or feast days. The Provincial Council of Tours (1583)[38] also requires a threefold publication, while those of Sorrento (1584),[39] Aix (1585),[40] Mexico (1585)[41] and Avignon (1594)[42] particularly stress the need of announcing in the parish church the forthcoming ordination at least a month before the ceremony.[43]

The party entrusted with this duty also makes a diligent inquiry

(14 vols., Coloniae Allobrogum, 1741), II, tit. *de scrutinio in ordine faciendo,* q. 1, n. 20; Passerini (1595-1677), *De Hominum Statibus et Officiis* (ed. emend., 3 vols., Lucae, 1732), III, quaest. CLXXXIX, art. X, nn. 800-6, 820-1.

[36] Quibus verbis patet, solius episcopi esse inquisitionem in vitam ac mores ordinandorum decernere, parochos vero ordinarios hujus rei inquisitores nuncupandos; quamvis si forte vel gratia, vel favor, vel inimicitia, vel aliquid aliud a parocho timeatur, quod recti iudicii vel quaesitionis legitimae rationem pervertere possit, inquirendi provincia aliis ad arbitrium episcopi demandari queat . . .—Hallier, *De Sacris Electionibus et Ordinationibus,* Pars. I, Sect. I, Cap. II, art. 3, n. 5.

[37] Cap. *de episcoporum officiis,* n. 2—Mansi, XXXIV A, 632.

[38] Tit. X—Mansi, XXXIV A, 822.

[39] C. XXVI, n.. 12—Mansi, XXXVI bis, 296.

[40] Tit. *quae ad sacramenti ordinis administrationem pertinent*—Mansi, XXXIV B, 961.

[41] Lib. I, tit. IV, n. 1—Mansi, XXXIV B, 1034.

[42] C. XIX—Mansi XXXIV B, 1341.

[43] Cf. Provincial Council of Besançon (1571), tit. *de examine ordinandorum*—Mansi, XXXVI bis, 62; Provincial Council of Cambrai (1586), tit. X—Mansi, XXXIV B, 1238.

of reliable sources concerning the natal origin, age,[44] character and life of the candidates. Reiffenstuel (1641-1703)[45] notes that, according to the prescription of the Council of Trent and the approved practice of the Church, the testimonials sent to the bishop by the pastor or other legitimate superior are based on knowledge gleaned from human observation. As long as there are no signs to the contrary, it is presumed that the necessary qualities are present.

The testimonial letters containing the results of the entire investigation are sent to the bishop as soon as possible.[46] Fermosini († 1672)[47] shows that these letters must give moral certitude to the bishop concerning the life and character of the ordinand. It is for this certainty that the Fourth Provincial Council of Milan (1576)[48] is striving when it deviates from the common law by demanding that the testimonial letters be forwarded shortly before ordination. This is supposed to give sufficient time for a thorough investigation and to provide against any change of status or character in the aspirant.

Besides these testimonial letters the candidate for sacred orders must also show that he possesses an ecclesiastical benefice sufficient to sustain him. If this is lacking, although the other requisites are present, orders may not be received.[49]

It is expected that the ones ordained to the subdiaconate and diaconate are able to live continently, will serve the churches to which they are assigned, and will realize, as becomes their station, the fitness of receiving Holy Communion, at least on Sundays and the solemn feasts.[50]

In candidates for the priesthood there is a consideration of whether or not they have faithfully conducted themselves in their former duties, and whether they are so conspicuous for piety and chastity as to give hope that they will be an example of good works.[51]

[44] Reiffenstuel, *Jus Canonicum,* lib. I, tit. XII, n. 15: . . . natales, atque aetate solent probari ex attestatione parochi, ac schedula baptismali.

[45] *Op. cit.*, n. 14.

[46] Conc. Trident., sess. XXIII, *de ref.*, c. 5.

[47] *Opera Omnia,* II, tit, *de scrutinio in ordine faciendo,* q. 1, n. 5.

[48] C. VII—Mansi, XXXIV A, 231.

[49] Conc. Trident., sess. XXI, *de ref.*, c. 2.

[50] *Ibid.*, sess. XXIII, *de ref.*, c. 13.

[51] *Ibid.*, c. 14.

B. *Constitution* Speculatores *to the Code of Canon Law*

1. *General Necessity for Testimonials*

The Constitution *Speculatores*[52] issued by Innocent XII (1691-1700) on November 4, 1694, is of importance, not because of the introduction of radically new legislation regarding the examination of ordinands, but because of insistence on and a clarification of the law of the Council of Trent. The main theme of the document is concerned with the proper bishop for ordination, but this has a necessary connection with testimonial letters.

Innocent XII decrees that a bishop who is the proper superior by reason of a benefice may ordain only if he has testimonial letters from the bishops who are proper superiors both by reason of origin and of domicile, on the parentage, age, character and life of the candidate. This attestation is preserved in the curia of the ordaining bishop.[53]

If there is a fortuitous element involved in birth so that, because of a journey, business, or some other temporary delay, a child is born away from the diocese which ordinarily is the place of origin, his place of origin is considered to be where the father permanently resides. In such a case, for ordination, testimonial letters are not required of the bishop of the place where the child is actually born. However, if such a period of time is passed there that a canonical impediment may possibly be contracted, the youth has to present to the ordaining bishop testimonial letters from the ordinary of the place of actual birth.[54] Caution in this regard is further stressed by the declaration that testimonials are obtained from the ordinary of

[52] *Fontes,* n. 258.

[53] *Ibid.,* § 3. Cf. Council of Rome (1725), tit. VI, c. IV—*Acta et Decreta Sacrorum Conciliorum Recentiorum, Collectio Lacensis* (7 vols., Friburgi Brisgoviae, 1870-1890), I, 355; Wernz, *Ius Decretalium,* II, n. 29 v; Gasparri, *De Sacra Ordinatione,* n. 726; Many († 1922), *Praelectiones de Sacra Ordinatione* (Parisiis, 1905), p. 309; Santi (1830-1885), *Praelectiones Iuris Canonici* (5 vols. in 3, Ratisbonae, 1904), lib. I, tit. 11, n. 39.

[54] Innocentius XII, const. *Speculatores,* 4 nov. 1694, § 4—*Fontes,* n. 258; Gasparri, *op. cit.,* nn. 728, 734; Many, *op. cit.,* p. 309; Santi, *loc. cit.*

the place of origin if residence continues there long enough to contract a canonical impediment.[55]

Even if the bishop has the right to ordain by reason of the candidate's association with the bishop as a member of the latter's household *(familiaritas)*,[56] testimonial letters are obtained from the bishop of origin and domicile.[57]

In the questions arising from this constitution the necessity of obtaining testimonials is frequently stressed. Thus the origin of a person in a given locality, and his reception of the sacrament of confirmation there along with the public announcement which seeks to ascertain the free status of the ordinand, indicate so prolonged a stay in a place that testimonial letters are required even though such a locality only incidentally constitutes the place of origin and not the domicile.[58]

Retention of a domicile by a father and the fact that a youth spends a notable part of his time there, even though born elsewhere, also engenders a need for testimonials from the ordinary of this parental domicile.[59] In a similar situation the passage of nine years in a city certainly is sufficient time for the contraction of an impediment and thus establishes a need for testimonial letters.[60]

Of special importance for the understanding of the Constitution *Speculatores* is an extensive explanation emanating from the Sacred Congregation of the Council. The case in question arises from a dispute regarding the nature of the following letter:

[55] Innocentius XII, *ibid.*, § 5.

[56] Cf. Conc. Trident., sess. XXIII, *de ref.*, c. 9.

[57] Innocentius XII, *ibid.*, § 6. Cf. Wernz, *loc. cit.;* Gasparri, *op. cit.*, n. 736; Many, *loc. cit.;* Santi, *loc. cit.;* McBride, *Incardination and Excardination of Seculars*, The Catholic University of America Canon Law Studies, n. 145 (Washington, D. C.: The Catholic University of America Press, 1941), p. 60. The last named author holds, contrary to the common opinion, that testimonial letters are obtained from one or the other of the previous proper bishops.

[58] S.C.C., *Neapolitana seu Vici Equen.*, 12 febr., 12 mart. 1718—*Fontes*, n. 3166.

[59] S.C.C., *Romana seu Tusculana*, 27 apr.. 1720—*Fontes*, n. 3206.

[60] S.C.C, *Asculana*, 7 febr. 1733—*Fontes*, n. 3399.

> Testamur Clericum Laurentium Meldicheschi nostrae Dioecesis in minoribus Ordinibus constitutum, nullo excommunicationis, irregularitatis, aut cujusvis alterius canonici impedimenti vinculo, saltem quod sciamus, innodatum existere, neque ullo crimine postulatum, sed esse bonis, et honestis moribus praeditum, ac talem, qualem in fortem Domini vocatos decet.[61]

A bishop, in accepting this testimonial, believes that it satisfies the Innocentian law, despite the absence of an attestation concerning the person's natal origin. In fact, this is thought unnecessary because it is indicated that the cleric has been promoted to minor orders.

On the other hand, the bishop issuing the letter denies that it is given with any thought of promotion to sacred orders. He considers it as nothing more than the usual commendation given to clerics leaving the diocese.

In the first solution the decision is that the letter is a testimonial sufficient for the person's rightful ordination by the extraneous bishop.[62] Less than a month later there is a reversal of this position.[63]

In adverting to the legislation of Innocent XII, the second answer notes that a testimony regarding the natal origin is omitted from the letter and that the reception of minor orders does not lessen the need for this testimonial. Moreover, the letter does not indicate that the cleric has attained the age required for major orders. It is true that proof of the requisite age may be adduced from other documents, but the testimony of the bishop, both of origin and domicile, is preferable. This obviates the possibility of fraud, since these bishops know the candidate, whereas another bishop may be deceived by false documents.

The reply continues by indicating that testimonials are sought of

[61] S.C.C., *Pientina, seu Ilcinen.*, 9 aug. 1733—*Thesaurus Resolutionum Sacrae Congregationis Concilii* (167 vols., Romae, 1718-1908), VI, 125.

[62] S.C.C., *Pientina, seu Ilcinen.*, 18 iul. 1733—*Thesaurus*, VI, 115. Cf. II Plenary Council of Baltimore (1866), tit. V, *De Sacramentis*, cap. VIII, *De Ordine*, nn. 320-1—*Concilii Plenarii Baltimorensis II, in Ecclesia Metropolitana Baltimorensi, a Die VII ad Diem XXI Octobris, A.D. MDCCCLXVI, Habiti, et a Sede Apostolica Recogniti, Acta et Decreta* (Baltimorae, 1868), p. 168.

[63] S.C.C., *Pientina, seu Ilcinen.*, 8 aug. 1733—*Thesaurus*, VI, 125.

the bishop of origin even if the candidate departs at an age eliminating the possibility of the contraction of an impediment. In such a case the bishop of origin is able to testify concerning the matter of the candidate's natal origin and present age.[64]

An additional point emphasized is that the original testimonial letter is not granted for the specific purpose of authorizing the candidate's elevation to the sacred orders. To say that a cleric fulfills the obligations of the minor orders is quite different from a declaration that he is suitable for a higher grade.[65]

It is the mind of the legislator that a testimonial on the life and character of the cleric be obtained from the bishop of origin and domicile. This is particularly necessary when it is a question of a new subject hitherto unknown to the bishop. To make certain that his character befits the sanctity of the grade of holy orders to which he aspires, it is expedient that testimonials, not of an absolute nature but pertinent to holy orders, be obtained. That such letters are secured is noted in the testimonial of ordination.

In further clarifying the nature of testimonial letters the Sacred Congregation of the Council declares that there is a great difference, on the one hand, between dimissorials which grant another bishop the faculty to promote a cleric to orders, and, on the other hand, testimonials which only bear witness to the fact that the cleric in question is worthy to receive orders.[66]

The testimonials given for the reception of orders also differ

[64] Cf. S.C.C., *Lunen.-Sarzanen.*, 29 maii 1824—*Fontes*, n. 3987. The later reply in this case stresses another aspect: the bishop of origin does not need dimissorials in order to ordain, but he does need testimonials if the ordinary of domicile is distinct from that of origin. Cf. Many, *De Sacra Ordinatione*, p. 318.

[65] Cf. Conc. Trident., sess. XXIII, *de ref.*, cc. 5. 7, 8, 12, 13; Hallier, *De Sacris Electionibus et Ordinationibus*, Pars. I, Sect. I, cap. II, 184-249; Gasparri, *De Sacra Ordinatione*, n. 717.

[66] S.C.C., *Pientina, seu Ilcinen.*, 8 aug. 1733—*Thesaurus*, VI, 125. Cf. *ASS*, XIV (1881), 398; Monacelli († 1714?), *Formularium Legale Practicum Fori Ecclesiastici* (3 vols., Venetiis, 1736-1751), I, tit. IV, formula III, IX; Gasparri, *op. cit.*, n. 706; Wernz, *Ius Decretalium*, II, n. 29; Many, *De Sacra Ordinatione*, p. 308; Schmalzgrueber, *Jus Ecclesiasticum*, lib. I, tit. 11, n. 50.

from those granted to a cleric when he is leaving the diocese.[67] If the last mentioned letters make no reference to ordination, fraud is inevitable if they are employed for this purpose.

The detailed reply of August 1733 is the most exhaustive study issued by the Sacred Congregation of the Council regarding testimonial letters. It does much to dissolve the ambiguity surrounding both the Tridentine and Innocentian legislation and, unlike its predecessor in July of the same year, is accepted as the confirmed norm.[68]

2. *Special Necessity for Testimonials*

a. *Possibility of Impediments*

In the latter half of the nineteenth century there are evidences of a special solicitude for situations in which impediments may be contracted. This is particularly true in the case of the military who frequently move from place to place. The question arises from a consideration of the length of time a soldier has to remain in a place in order to need testimonials from the ordinary of that place declaring that he is free of canonical impediments.

In solving this difficulty the Sacred Congregation of the Council notes that the dispositions of the Constitutions *Speculatores* and *Apostolicae Sedis* are still operative. As a consequence, a bishop is not free to promote his own subjects to holy orders if they spend so great a period of time in another diocese that a canonical impediment may be contracted. The bishop must have testimonial letters from the ordinary of the place where the *clerical* soldier resides for three months.[69] Thus, there is extended to secular clerics, and given the force of general law, the discipline applicable in the case of re-

[67] S.C.C., *loc. cit.;* Monacelli, *op. cit.,* formula VI; Wernz, *loc. cit.:* Litterae igitur dimissoriae distinguuntur a litteris *excardinationis,* quibus quis e clero dioecesis dimittitur, a litteris *commendatitiis,* quae clericis peregre profecturis conceduntur, a *testimonio* de ordinibus rite receptis, denique a litteris *testimonialibus,* quae exhibent testimonium authenticum de honesta vita, scientia, immunitate ordinandi ab omni impedimento canonico ad ordines recipiendos.

[68] S.C.C., *Burgi, S. Domnini seu Cremonen.,* 1 aug. 1750—*Thesaurus,* XIV, 137; *Fontes,* n. 3611.

[69] S.C.C., *Firmana,* 9 sept. 1893—*Fontes,* n. 4288. Cf. Wernz, *Ius Decretalium,* II, n. 29 v; Many, *De Sacra Ordinatione,* p. 311.

ligious returning from the army.[70] The secret vigilance which a bishop is instructed to exercise over clerics in the army is not an acceptable substitute for these letters.[71]

Outside the case of the military, the practice of the Roman Curia, the intention of the common law, and the teaching of the doctors set a residence of six months as the period begetting a necessity for testimonials.[72]

In the computation of this time the period is considered to be a moral unit. However, there is nothing to prevent the bishop from inquiring about the suitableness of the candidate and from requiring testimonials for a shorter or non-continuous period, or from demanding a suppletory oath if this is deemed necessary.[73] In general, the spirit rather than the letter of the law is followed,[74] and consideration is given to the fact that the law contemplates what generally happens in determining a definite time as a likely space for the contraction of an impediment. In the abstract, the shortest possible period suffices.[75]

In the event that a bishop is unable to grant testimonial letters for the reason that the candidate is unknown, the Apostolic See is accustomed to concede to the curia the faculty of supplying for this deficiency by allowing a suppletory oath to be taken.[76] In an exceptional case the bishops of Austria are given the faculty for ten years to confer orders if, in a particular case, there is grave difficulty in obtaining testimonials and if they are morally certain of the suitability of the ordinand.[77]

Unless a canonical impediment does exist, the bishop is not to

[70] S.C. Ep. et Reg., instr. 27 nov. 1892, n. 5—*Fontes,* n. 2021.

[71] S.C.S. Off., instr. 16 sept. 1875—*Fontes,* n. 1045. Cf. *Il Monitore Ecclesiastico* (Romae, 1876—), VIII (1893), Pars I, pp. 169-70; XVI (1904), 247.

[72] S.C.C., *Urgellen.,* 26 ian. 1895—*Fontes,* n. 4293.

[73] S.C.C., *Pragen.,* 25 iun. 1904—*Fontes,* n. 4318.

[74] S.C.C., *Urgellen.,* 26 ian. 1895—*Fontes,* n. 4293.

[75] S.C.C., *Pragen.,* 25 iun. 1904—*Fontes,* n. 4318.

[76] S.C.C., *Urgellen.,* 26 ian. 1895—*Fontes,* n. 4293.

[77] *Archiv für katholisches Kirchenrecht* (Innsbruck, 1857-1861; Mainz, 1862—), LXXV (1895), 128.

refuse to grant these attestations.[78] Otherwise it would be in the power of one bishop to interfere with the rights of another.[79] In such a difficulty recourse is had to the Holy See.[80]

On Ferbuary 25, 1896, the Congregation for the Propagation of the Faith instructs candidates coming from Poland to the United States to present testimonials from this Congregation.[81] These letters attest to their permission to leave the diocese, their freedom from censures, and their good character. However, this provision is found to be short-lived, being supplanted by the legislation of July 20, 1898,[82] of December 22, 1905,[83] and of November 24, 1906.[84] These decrees effect no change in the ordinary law on testimonial letters.

b. *Religious Candidates*

The general law of the Council of Trent is that regulars are not ordained without an examination by the bishop.[85] This is understood as restricted to the examination on requisite knowledge and instruction so that the investigation of the other qualities of the ordinand is left to the regular superiors.[86]

Shortly after the Council of Trent the Sacred Congregation of the Council declares that the superiors of regulars may grant dimissorials for their subjects if these subjects have the qualities required for the reception of orders.[87] These dimissorials are considered so

[78] S.C. Ep. et Reg., *Sever.*, 13 mart. 1701; S.C.C., *Neapolit., seu Hyeracen.*, 27 iul. 1699; *Neapol. seu Scal.*, 19 febr. 1701—S.C. Ep. et Reg., *Verulana, Aquinaten. et Neapolitana*, 16 iul. 1841—Bizzarri, *Collectanea in Usum Secretariae Sacrae Congregationis Episcoporum et Regularium* (Romae, 1885), p. 474.

[79] *Loc. cit.*

[80] S.C.C., *Rhemen.*, 21 apr. 1668—Bizzarri, *op. cit.*, p. 475.

[81] *Collectanea S. Congregationis de Propaganda Fide* (2 vols., Romae, 1907), n. 1918.

[82] S.C.C., decr. *A primis—Fontes*, n. 4307.

[83] S.C.C., decr. *Vetuit—Fontes*, n. 4327.

[84] S.C.C., decr.—*Fontes*, n. 4330.

[85] Sess. XXIII, *de ref.*, c. 12.

[86] Cf. Piatus Montensis (1815-1904), *Praelectiones Iuris Regularis* (ed. 3, 2 vols., Tornaci, 1906), II, Q. 364.

[87] S.C.C., decr. 15 mart. 1596—*Fontes*, n. 2294.

effective that other testimonials from the ordinary of origin are unnecessary.[88]

In the history of the legislation governing the ordination of regulars, considerable controversy exists regarding the privileges of the religious and the right to ordain of the bishop in whose diocese the house of the religious is situated.[89] In contrast, there seems to be no question of the right of the superior to testify concerning the existence of the required qualities in the candidate. He makes such an attestation when granting dimissorials.[90]

The important governing norm in this aspect of the legislation is the Constitution *Impositi Nobis*,[91] issued by Benedict XIV (1740-1758) on February 27, 1747. The Holy Father herein confirms and orders observance of the law made in this matter by his predecessors Gregory XIII (1572-1585), Sixtus V (1585-1590), Clement VIII (1592-1605) and Innocent XIII (1721-1724). To their declaration he adds the condition that the dimissorials of regular superiors, if directed to a bishop outside the diocese, lack meaning unless there is attached an authentic declaration of the vicar-general, the chancellor, or the secretary of the diocesan bishop. This attestation certifies that the bishop of the diocese in which the religious house is situated is absent from the diocese or that he is not going to impose hands at the next time indicated by law for the conferring of orders.[92]

Later pontiffs are content to emphasize specific points. They do not effect any change in this law. Thus, it is stressed that professed religious of simple or solemn vows are not admitted to sacred orders unless they have testimonials proving the study of theology for a year, if there be question of ordination to the subdiaconate, for two years, with reference to the diaconate, and for at least three years, in relation to the priesthood.[93]

[88] S.C.C., *Senonen.*, 28 febr. 1654, ad 9—*Fontes*, n. 2734.

[89] Cf. Moeder, *The Proper Bishop for Ordination and Dimissorial Letters*, The Catholic University of America Canon Law Studies, n. 95 (Washington, D. C.: The Catholic University of America, 1935), pp. 32-7.

[90] Cf. Wernz, *Ius Decretalium*, II, n. 29 v.

[91] *Fontes*, n. 376.

[92] Const. *Impositi Nobis*, § 12—*Fontes*, n. 376.

[93] S.C. Ep. et Reg., decr. *Auctis admodum*, 4 nov. 1892, n. 6—Fontes, n. 2020.

Leo XIII (1878-1903), in prescribing for the general observance of the law concerning ordinations, demands, particularly in the case of institutes of simple vows approved by the Holy See, that the aspirants be provided with proper testimonials.[94]

This tendency toward a precise expression in the testimonials of the qualities of the candidate is also evident in a declaration of the Sacred Congregation of Religious.[95] This declaration requires that in the testimonials there be given by the superiors data on (a) the course in theology: that the candidate from such a year, month and day, to such a year, month and day, and in such a school, undertook the theological studies necessary for the orders for which he is presented, and that he is found worthy in a final examination; (b) the inferior studies: (i) that the same candidate, having correctly finished the primary studies, completed the study of letters in such a school, for so many academic years, and passed the final examination; (ii) that the same candidate, after properly finishing the study of letters, mastered the entire course of philosophy in such a school, for so many academic years, and passed the final examination.

These are requisites applicable throughout the world, embracing not only religious congregations with vows but also those institutes whose members are bound by a simple promise of perseverance.[96]

c. *Commission by the Bishop to Investigate*

In the period between the Constitution *Speculatores* and the Code, the general law governing those commissioned by the bishop

[94] Const. *Conditae a Christo,* 8 dec. 1900—*Fontes,* n. 644.

[95] 7 sept. 1909, ad VIII—*Fontes,* n. 4397. Cf. *Periodica de Re Canonica et Morali utili Praesertim Religiosis et Missionariis* (Brugis, 1905—), V (1913), (24)-(28), 46-8.

[96] S.C. de Religiosis, 31 maii 1910, ad 2—*Fontes,* n. 4402. In sharp contrast to this general provision is the prior and particular legislation of the provincial Council of Tuam (1817): Nullus dehinc ad sacros ordines promoveatur, nisi authenticum instrumentum habeat, se cursum theologicum duorum saltem annorum in aliqua academia perfecisse. Quod regulares vero, qui se praesentant ut sacros ordines recipiant, requiritur solummodo, ut in catechismo ad ordinandos examinentur, et ab Ordinario approbentur. Praeterea litteras sui provincialis exhibeant, attestantes, sic praesentatos statim post ordinationem mittendos esse vel ad collegium aliquod transmarinum, vel domi instruendos.—*Coll. Lac.,* III, 766 d.

to investigate remains unchanged.[97] The only adaptations are the specifications of particular legislators.

In many places a custom contrary to the law of announcing forthcoming ordinations is in possession.[98] However, this phase of the law receives special attention in some of the councils. There is a general demand, as in the provincial councils of Avignon (1849),[99] Sens (1850),[100] Bourges (1850)[101] and Westminster (1852),[102] that this publication be made, and that observance be restored where desuetude has usurped the place of the law. Ordinarily the name of the candidate and the manifestation of his desire are announced on three feast days.[103]

The inquiry of the pastor or of some other suitable person covers the matters connected with the parentage, the present age, the moral character and life of the ordinand.[104] Testimonials, as required by common law, are forwarded to the bishop as soon as possible.

Article III. *Second Examination of the Candidate*

A. *General Necessity*

The second examination of the candidate for orders is that

[97] Cf. Conc. Trident., sess. XXIII, *de ref.*, c. 5.

[98] Cf. Schmalzgrueber, *Ius Ecclesiasticum Universum,* lib. I, tit. 12, n. 1; Reiffenstuel, *Jus Canonicum Universum,* lib. I, tit. 12, n. 3; Gasparri, *De Sacra Ordinatione,* n. 701; Many, *De Sacra Ordinatione,* p. 306.

[99] Cap. VII, n. 4—*Coll. Lac.,* IV, 341.

[100] Cap. VII—*Coll. Lac.,* IV, 893.

[101] *Coll. Lac.,* IV, 1118.

[102] Tit. XXI—*Coll. Lac.,* III, 936.

[103] Cf. Provincial Council of Naples (1699), *Instructio pro ordinandis*—Mansi, XXXVI ter, 824; Holy Synod of Mt. Lebanon (1736)—*Coll. Lac.,* II, 239; Provincial Council of Auch (1851), tit. VI, n. XCVII—*Coll. Lac.,* IV, 1189.

[104] Cf. Pius X (1903-1914), ep. encyl. *Iucunda sane,* 12 mart. 1904—*ASS,* XXXVI (1903-1904), 526; epist. *La ristorazione,* 5 maii 1904—*Fontes,* n. 661; Provincial Council of Naples, *loc. cit.;* Council of the Ruthenians (1720), n. VII—Mansi, XXXV B, 1501; Provincial Council of Embrun (1727), cap. XIII—*Coll. Lac.,* I, 632; Provincial Council of Avignon (1849), cap. VII—*Coll. Lac.,* IV, 341; Provincial Council of Toulouse (1850), n. XIII—*Coll. Lac.,* IV, 1036; I Provincial Council of Cincinnati (1855), n. IV—*Coll. Lac.,* III, 195; II Plenary Council of Baltimore (1866), n. 322—*Acta et Decreta,* p. 169.

which the Council of Trent prescribed in chapter 7 of its twenty-third session, on reformation:

> Sancta synodus antiquorum canonum vestigiis inhaerendo decernit, ut, quando episcopus ordinationem facere disposuerit, omnes, qui ad sacrum ministerium accedere voluerint, feria quarta ante ipsam ordinationem, vel quando episcopo videbitur, ad civitatem evocentur. Episcopus autem, sacerdotibus et aliis prudentibus viris peritis divinae legis ac in ecclesiasticis sanctionibus exercitatis sibi adscitis, ordinandorum genus, personam, aetatem, institutionem, mores, doctrinam et fidem diligenter investiget et examinet.

This chapter of the Council of Trent is itself rooted in the ancient law of the Church, being taken almost verbatim from the *Decretum Gratiani.* [105]

As Pius X (1908-1914)[106] points out, this law particularly means that no one desirous of promotion to sacred orders is excused from submitting to a doctrinal examination. Moreover, this examination is not a mere formality but a diligent investigation, since the intellectual equipment of the candidate rivals in importance the necessity of his having a good character.

The holding of the examination, as Fermosini († 1672),[107] Giraldi (1692-1775),[108] Wigandt († 1708),[109] Reiffenstuel (1641-1703),[110] and Many († 1922)[111] indicate, is an actual necessity for all orders to determine the presence or absence of qualities required in the candidates. As before the Council of Trent, so also subsequent

105 C. 5, D. XXIV—Council of Nantes, cap. XI—Mansi, XVIII a, 169.

106 Motu propr., *Sacrosancta Tridentina Synodus,* 16 iul. 1905—*ASS,* XXXVIII (1905-1906), 8 s.

107 *Opera Omnia,* II, tit. *de scrutinio in ordine faciendo,* q. 1, n. 13.

108 *Expositio Juris Pontificii* (2 vols., Romae, 1829-1830), Pars II, t. III, sect. XCIV, ad sess. XXIII, c. 7.

109 *Tribunal Confessariorum et Ordinandorum* (Venetiis, 1717), tract. XV, *de sacramento ordinis,* ex. I.

110 *Jus Canonicum,* lib. I, tit. 12, nn. 6-16.

111 *De Sacra Ordinatione,* p. 294.

to it, the popes[112] and particular councils[113] insist on it that the ministers of the Church be worthy, pious, continent, and faithful in the fulfillment of their duties. In this regard it is not sufficient that the bishop merely know of no evil in the ordinand. The examination is held in order that moral certitude may be obtained concerning "the parentage, person, age, title, character, learning and faith of those who are to be ordained."[114]

In the actual observance of the general prescript, Gasparri (1852-1934)[115] notes that it is the practice for the chancellor or another priest deputed by the bishop to gather together all the testimonies so that the required examination is reduced to an inquiry into the knowledge of the candidate.

The Council of Trent does not go beyond the general statement of the matter for the examination, but the significance of the various items enumerated may be understood from the meanings assigned by the commentators.

Genus: the candidate must be born of Catholic parents, be legitimate, and be baptized;[116]

[112] Cf. Clemens VIII, const. *Dives in misericordia,* 20 aug. 1599—*Bullarum Diplomatum et Privilegiorum Sanctorum Pontificum* Editio Taurinensis (24 vols., Augustae Taurinorum, 1857-1872), X, 526; Innocentius XIII, const. *Apostolici ministerii,* 23 maii 1723—*Fontes,* n. 280; Pius X, motu propr. *Religisorum Ordinum,* 19 mart. 1906—*Fontes,* n. 673.

[113] Cf. Provincial Council of Ravenna (1568), tit. *de ordine*—Mansi, XXXV A, 622; Provincial Council of Mexico (1585), lib. I, tit. IV—Mansi, XXXIV B, 1032; Provincial Council of Bordeaux (1850), cap. IV—*Coll. Lac.,* IV, 597; Provincial Council of Toulouse (1850), tit. XIII—*Coll. Lac.,* IV, 1036; Provincial Council of Auch (1851), tit. 6—*Coll. Lac.,* IV, 1189; Plenary Council of Latin America (1899), tit. V, cap. VII—*Acta et Decreta Concilii Plenarii Americae Latinae in Urbe Celebrati, A.D. MDCCCXCIX* (2 vols., Romae, 1902-1910), I, nn. 578-80.

[114] Conc. Trident., sess. XXIII, *de ref.,* c. 7. The wording of this part of the chapter is very similar to that of chapter 5, which speaks of an investigation "de ipsorum ordinandorum natalibus, aetate, moribus et vita. . ."

[115] *De Sacra Ordinatione,* n. 755.

[116] Barbosa, *Collectanea Doctorum,* ad sess. XXIII, c. 7; Fermosini, *Opera Omia,* II, tit. *de scrutinio in ordine faciendo,* q. I, n. 8; Reiffenstuel, *Jus Canonicum,* lib. I, tit. 12, n. 6; Schmalzgrueber, *Jus Ecclesiasticum,* lib. I, tit. 12, n. 2; Engel, *Collegium Universi Iuris Canonici,* tit. 12; Gasparri, *De Sacra Ordinatione,* n. 755; Many, *De Sacra Ordinatione,* p. 295.

Persona: he must be free of impediments and irregularities;[117]

Aetas: his age must conform to the legal requirements;[118]

Institutio: the ordinand must have a proper title for ordination;[119]

Doctrina: his learning must correspond to the order the candidate desires to receive;[120]

Mores: the suitableness of the one seeking ordination must be known through the testimonials forwarded to the bishop;[121]

Fides: the candidate must be well-grounded in the faith.[122]

In the investigation of these qualities the right of the bishop to examine is primary, but the practical difficulty involved in a personal survey of the candidates permits him to call to his assistance "priests and other prudent men skilled in the divine law and experienced in the laws of the Church. . ."[123] This is a norm employed in the selection of the examiners, but it begets no obligation to select for this purpose either synodal examiners or the archdeacon.[124]

The bishops of the United States are fully aware of the importance of this legislation, for in the Second Plenary Council of

[117] Auctores citati, *loc. cit.*

[118] Reiffenstuel, *loc. cit.;* Schmalzgrueber, *loc. cit.;* Gasparri, *loc. cit.;* Many, *op. cit.*, p. 297.

[119] Barbosa, *loc. cit.;* Fermosini, *loc. cit.;* Gasparri, *loc. cit.;* Schmalzgrueber, *loc. cit.* Many teaches that *institutio* refers to the education of the aspirant. Cf. *loc. cit.*

[120] Auctores citati, *loc. cit.*

[121] Reiffenstuel, *op. cit.*, n. 13; Schmalzgrueber, *loc. cit.;* Engel, *loc. cit.;* Gasparri., *loc. cit.;* Many, *loc. cit.;* Fermosinus, *loc. cit.*

[122] Many, *op. cit.*, p. 298.

[123] Conc. Trident., sess. XXIII, *de ref.*, c. 7; Benedictus XIV, *De Synodo Dioecesana,* V, cap. 2, n. 2; Fermosini, *Opera Omnia,* II, tit. *de scrutinio in ordine faciendo,* q. I, n. 4; Wigandt, *Tribunal Confessariorum et Ordinandorum,* tract. XV, *de sacramento ordinis,* ex. I; Gasparri, *De Sacra Ordinatione,* nn. 747, 754; Many, *De Sacra Ordinatione,* p. 295.

[124] S.C. Ep. et Reg., *Iadren.*, 17 sept. 1660—*Fontes,* n. 1794. Cf. Synod of the Province of Gniezno (Gnesen, 1577)—Mansi, XXXVI bis, 675; Provincial Council of Mexico (1585), lib. I, tit. IV—Mansi, XXXIV B, 1037; Provincial Council of Benevento (1599), tit. XXVI—Mansi, XXXVI bis, 441; Council of Ruthenians (1720), n. VII—Mansi, XXXV B, 1500; I Provincial Council of Cincinnati (1855), tit. IV—*Coll. Lac.*, III, 195.

Baltimore (1866)[125] they stress the need of appointing four, or at least three, such examiners in the dioceses of the provinces. Then, in the Third Plenary Council of Baltimore (1884)[126] the Tridentine law is appealed to specifically, and it is decided that examiners are to be appointed for the purpose, among other things, of examining ordinands.

In completing the consideration of the general necessity of this examination one must note that the testimonials of regular superiors are an adequate voucher for the qualities of the candidate, with the exception that regular ordinands must submit to an investigation of their learning by the ordaining bishop.[127] However there is a dispute regarding the obligations of the recipient of such an attestation. Petra (1662-1747),[128] Riganti (1661-1735),[129] Bouix (1808-1870)[130] and Gasparri[131] maintain that the bishop must examine the candidate despite the assurances given by the regular superior. On the other

[125] Tit. V, *De Sacramentis,* cap. VIII, *De Ordine,* n. 316—*Acta et Decreta,* p. 167.

[126] Tit. II, *De Personis Ecclesiasticis,* cap. III, *De Examinatoribus Cleri Dioecesani,* n. 24—*Acta et Decreta Concilii Plenarii Baltimorensis Tertii, A.D. MDCCCLXXXIV* (Baltimorae, 1886), p. 18.

[127] Conc. Trident., sess. XXIII, *de ref.,* c. 12; Innocentius XIII, const. *Apostolici ministerii,* 23 maii 1723, § 5—*Fontes,* n. 280; Benedictus XIII, const. *In supremo,* 23 sept. 1724, §§ 4, 28—*Fontes,* n. 283; const. *Pastoralis officii,* 27 mart. 1726, § 3—*Fontes,* n. 292; Benedictus XIV, const. *Impositi Nobis,* 27 febr. 1747—*Fontes,* n. 376; Pius X, motu propr. *Religiosorum Ordinum,* 19 mart. 1906—*Fontes,* n. 673; S.C. Ep. et Reg., *Ordinis Eremitarum Camaldulensium,* 13 iul. 1730—*Fontes,* n. 1847; S.C.C., decr. 15 mart. 1596—*Fontes,* n. 2294. Cf. Monacelli, *Formularium,* II, tit. XIII, formula IV, n. 28; Fermosini, *Opera Omnia,* II, tit. *de scrutinio in ordine faciendo,* q. I, nn. 19-20; Gasparri, *De Sacra Ordinatione,* n. 753; Santi, *Praelectiones,* lib. I, tit. 12, n. 2; Prümmer (1866-1931), *Ius Regularium Speciale* (Friburgi Brisgoviae, 1907), n. 236; Piatus Montensis, *Praelectiones,* II, Q. 364.

[128] *Commentaria ad Constitutiones Apostolicas* (5 vols., Venetiis, 1729), II, Const. un. Urbani II, n. 44.

[129] *Commentaria in Regulas, Constitutiones et Ordinationes Cancellariae Apostolicae* (4 vols. in 2, Coloniae Allobrogum, 1751), In regulam 24 Canc. § 3, n. 283.

[130] *Tractatus de Episcopo* (ed. 2, 2 vols., Parisiis, 1873), II, 209.

[131] *Loc. cit.*

hand, Piat (1815-1904),[132] Passerini (1595-1677)[133] and Many († 1922)[134] hold that this attestation is acceptable inasmuch as the bishop, as all agree, need not do the examining himself, and a bishop ordaining in virtue of a dimissorial letter is not obliged to examine the candidate, but may accept the testimony of the religious superior.

B. *Specific Considerations*

The general requirement for ordination is that the candidate know what the very nature of the order demands. Beyond this the Council of Trent[135] prescribes that the one desirous of tonsure be instructed in the rudiments of the faith and that he be able to read and write. Ordinarily, this minimal requirement is accepted as sufficient.[136] In particular instances special norms must be satisfied. Thus the Provincial Council of Sorrento (1584)[137] decrees that, in the examination, the ordinand show his knowledge of the ordinary book of Christian doctrine.

For reception of the minor orders there is insistence on knowledge of the Latin language.[138] As with tonsure, this is the standard requirement after the Council of Trent,[139] and the only notable varia-

[132] *Op. cit.*, II, 286.

[133] *De Hominum Statibus et Officiis*, q. CLXXXIX, art. X, n. 821.

[134] *De Sacra Ordinatione*, p. 393.

[135] Sess. XXIII, *de ref.*, c. 4. Cf. Barbosa, *Collectanea Doctorum*, ad sess. XXIII, c. 4; Fermosini, *Opera Omnia*, tit. *de scrutinio in ordine faciendo*, q. I, n. 12; Engel, *Collegium Universi Iuris Canonici*, lib. I, tit. 12; Reiffenstuel, *Jus Canonicum*, lib. I, tit. 11, n. 66; Schmalzgrueber, *Jus Ecclesiasticum*, lib. I, tit. 11, n. 28; Ferraris (†ca.1763), *Prompta Bibliotheca Canonica, Juridico-Moralis Theologica* (8 vols., Bononiae, 1746), V, "Ordo, Ordinare," art. II, n. 80; Wernz, *Ius Decretalium*, II, n. 117; Gasparri, *De Sacra Ordinatione*, n. 558; Fabius Incarnatus, *Scrutinium Sacerdotale* (Venetiis, 1708), pp. 1-9.

[136] Provincial Council of Besançon (1571), tit. *de examine ordinandorum*, n. 4—Mansi, XXXVI bis, 62; Provincial Council of Bordeaux (1583), tit. XIV—Mansi, XXXIV A, 760; Provincial Council of Aquileia (1596), n. XI —Mansi, XXXIV B, 1400; National Synod of Albania (1703)—*Coll. Lac.*, I, 306.

[137] Tit. XXVI, n. 21—Mansi, XXXV bis, 296.

[138] Conc. Trident., sess. XXIII, *de ref.*, c. 11.

[139] Cf. Provincial Council of Besançon, *ibid.* n. 5; Provincial Council of Aquileia, *loc. cit.;* Synod of Bahia (1707)—*Coll. Lac.*, I, 851.

tion is that which is introduced by the Provincial Council of Mexico (1585).[140] This council expects that the candidate also be versed in ecclesiastical chant.

Among commentators there is a strong difference of opinion regarding the interpretation of the common law of the Council of Trent. Some[141] demand faithful adherence to it, while others[142] teach that the minor orders may be conferred on one who does not know Latin, provided only that the candidate has the ability to learn it.

The aspirant to the subdiaconate must be versed in letters and in what pertains to the exercise of this order.[143] This general statement is not particularized in Tridentine law, but some of the provincial councils enlarge on it by demanding knowledge of grammar,[144] chant,[145] the catechism,[146] the divine office,[147] the sacred rites[148] and a tract in theology.[149]

In prescribing for the diaconate the Council of Trent[150] does

---

[140] Lib. I, tit. IV—Mansi, XXXIV B, 1032.

[141] Lambertini (postea Benedictus XIV), *Institutiones Ecclesiasticae* (Romae, 1747), n. XLII, p. 216; S. Alphonsus Liguori (1696-1787), *Theologia Moralis* (ed. absolutissima, 9 vols., Vesontione, 1832), VII, n. 790; Gasparri, *De Sacra Ordinatione,* n. 122; Many, *De Sacra Ordinatione,* p. 231.

[142] Barbosa, *Collectanea Doctorum,* ad sess. XXIII, c. 11; Fermosini, *Opera Omnia,* II, tit. *de scrutinio in ordine faciendo,* q. I, n. 12.

[143] Conc. Trident., sess. XXIII, *de ref.,* c. 13; Innocentius XIII, const. *Apostolici ministerii,* 23 maii 1723, § 5—*Fontes,* n. 280; *Benedictus* XIII, const. *In supremo,* 23 sept. 1724, § 28—*Fontes,* n. 283; Benedictus XIV, const. *Impositi Nobis,* 27 febr. 1747, § 8—*Fontes,* n. 376.

[144] Provincial Council of Besançon (1571), tit. *de examine ordinandorum*—Mansi, XXXVI bis, 62

[145] *Loc. cit.;* Provincial Council of Mexico (1585), lib. I, tit. IV—Mansi, XXXIV B, 1033; Provincial Synod of Benevento (1693), tit. VI, cap VIII—*Coll. Lac.,* I, 30.

[146] Provincial Council of Besançon (1571), *loc. cit.;* Provincial Council of Sorrento (1584), tit. XXVI—Mansi, XXXV bis, 296.

[147] Provincial Council of Bordeaux (1583)—Mansi, XXXIV A, 759; Provincial Council of Mexico, *loc. cit.;* National Synod of Albania (1703)—*Coll. Lac.,* I, 306.

[148] Provincial Synod of Benevento, *loc. cit.*

[149] Provincial Council of Westminster (1852), tit. XXI—*Coll. Lac.,* III, 936. Cf. Gasparri, *De Sacra Ordinatione,* n. 756.

[150] Conc. Trident., sess. XXIII, *de ref.,* c. 13. Cf. Innocentius XIII, *loc. cit.;* Benedictus XIII, *loc. cit.;* Benedictus XIV, *loc. cit.*

not go beyond the same general requirement already noted for the subdiaconate. The candidate for the diaconate is also to be conversant with letters and what is essential for the exercise of the order. The specifications of this law tend to demand a knowledge of grammar,[151] chant,[152] the catechism,[153] the breviary,[154] ceremonies[155] and two tracts in theology.[156]

For elevation to the priesthood it is required that the ordinand be able "to teach the people those things which are necessary for all to know for salvation and to administer the sacraments. . ."[157] This is the precept of the Council of Trent. Innocent XIII enlarges on it by demanding skill in moral theology[158] and both Benedict XIII[159] and Benedict XIV[160] demand observance of the Innocentian law.

In particular conciliar legislation there frequently appear instructions more explicit than those of the common law. The Provincial Synod of Benevento (1693)[161] requires that the ordinand know the sacred rites and Gregorian chant; the conciliar fathers of Mexico[162] declare that Mass is not to be said unless the examination of the master of ceremonies has been passed; the Provincial Councils

[151] Provincial Council of Besançon, *loc. cit.*

[152] *Loc. cit.;* Provincial Council of Sorrento, *loc. cit.;* Provincial Synod of Benevento, *loc. cit.*

[153] Provincial Council of Besançon, *loc. cit.;* Provincial Council of Sorrento, *loc. cit.*

[154] Provincial Council of Besançon, *loc. cit.*

[155] Provincial Council of Mexico, *loc. cit.;* Provincial Synod of Benevento, *loc. cit.*

[156] Provincial Council of Westminster (1852), tit. XXI—*Coll. Lac.*, III, 936. Cf. Gasparri, *De Sacra Ordinatione*, nn. 756-7.

[157] Conc. Trident., sess. XXIII, *re ref.*, c. 14.

[158] Innocentius XIII, const. *Apostolici ministerii*, 23 maii 1723, § 5—*Fontes*, n. 280.

[159] Const. *In supremo*, 23 sept. 1724, § 28—*Fontes*, n. 283.

[160] Const. *Impositi Nobis*, 27 febr. 1747, § 8—*Fontes*, n. 376.

[161] Tit. VI, cap. VIII—*Coll. Lac.*, I, 30.

[162] Provincial Council of Mexico (1585), lib. I, tit. IV—Mansi, XXXIV B, 1032.

both of Mexico[163] and Rome[164] legislate that those having the care of souls must also be approved for administering the sacrament of penance and must be able to explain the gospel.[165]

Article IV. *Sanctions*

In emphasizing the desirability of ordination by one's own bishop, the Council of Trent decrees that "if anyone should ask to be promoted by another, this shall under no condition, even under the pretext of any general or special rescript or privilege, even at the times specified, be permitted him unless his probity and morals be recommended by the testimony of his ordinary. Otherwise the one ordaining shall be suspended for a year from conferring orders, and the one ordained shall be suspended from exercising the orders received for as long a period as his ordinary shall see fit."[166]

A reason for this insistence is found in the practice whereby certain bishops without sees presume to confer orders indiscriminately on candidates lacking commendatory letters from the proper authorities.[167] The result of this is that the less suitable, those who lack knowledge both of the temporal and spiritual, and those who have been rejected by their own bishop as unqualified and unworthy are ordained. For such a procedure the council decrees a suspension *ipso iure* for one year for the ordaining prelate, while the recipient of orders is suspended for as long as his ordinary deems fit. In fact, those who are promoted by any authority whatsoever without the previous examination and commendatory letters of their bishop can be suspended from the exercise of their orders, if their own bishop finds them unfit to celebrate the divine offices and to administer

[163] *Loc. cit.*

[164] Council of Rome (1725), tit. VI, cap. III—*Coll. Lac.*, I, 354. Cf. Wigandt, *Tribunal Confessariorum et Ordinandorum*, tract. XV, ex. V, p. 633.

[165] Note: For a particularly detailed outline of the matter and form for the examination of ordinands cf. V Provincial Council of Milan (1579), Pars III, tit. II, *De examinandi ratione* (Mansi, XXXIV A, 431-43) and the Provincial Council of Naples (1699), tit. XVII, *Instructio pro ordinandis*, III, *De scientia ordinandorum* (Mansi, XXXVI ter, 825). A thorough study of these provisions is beyond the scope of this work, but it is noteworthy that their legislation is fundamentally the same as that of the Council of Trent.

[166] Conc. Trident., sess. XXIII, *de ref.*, c. 8.

[167] *Ibid.*, sess. XIV, *de ref.*, c. 2.

the sacraments.[168] This law is applicable even though the candidates are found to be qualified and are approved by the ordaining prelate. However, it does not extend to the predecessors of the proper bishop.[169]

Shortly after the Council of Trent, in the Constitution *Sanctum et salutare*[170] of January 5, 1589, Sixtus V (1585-1590) points out how solicitous the Church always is concerning the honorable parentage, the requisite age, the laudable life, character, sanctity, knowledge and other qualities required in ordinands. After noting the unfortunate situation whereby the unqualified and the unworthy are ordained without regard for the specified examination and approbation, this pontiff demands observance of the law. To give force to his utterance he decrees that the penalty for a violation of the legislation on ordinations is suspension from conferring orders, even first tonsure, and the exercise of all pontificals, interdiction of entry in a church, and the infliction of other grave penalties to be determined by the reigning pope. Disregard for these sanctions is to bring on the additional penalties of suspension from rule and administration of the church, and from the reception of any fruits of a benefice. Remission of the penalties is reserved to the Roman pontiff.[171]

By the time of his pontificate Clement VIII (1592-1605)[172] notes that the fear of these sanctions is so great that bishops are inclined to be scrupulous in ordaining. The result is that a great diminution in the number of priests and clerics is evident is some places. Consequently, this pontiff moderates the penalties of Sixtus V so as to restore to their vigor the legislation of Pius II (1458-1464)[173] and the ordinances of the Tridentine decree.[174]

In the Constitution *Speculatores*[175] Innocent XII (1691-1700)

[168] *Ibid.*, c. 3.

[169] Cf. Fagnanus, *Commentaria*, ad c. 13, X, *de aetate et qualitate et ordine praeficiendorum*, I, n. 16.

[170] *Fontes*, n. 166.

[171] Cf. S.C. Ep. et Reg., *Vestana*, 25 maii 1594—*Fontes*, n. 1508.

[172] Const. *Romanum Pontificem*, 28 febr. 1596—*Fontes*, n. 182.

[173] Const. *Cum ex sacrorum*, 17 nov. 1461—*Fontes*, n. 57.

[174] Cf. Barbosa, *Collectanea Doctorum*, ad sess. XXIII, c. 12.

[175] 4 nov. 1694—*Fontes*, n. 258.

provides against the possibility of fraud by the ordinand. If the testimonial letters do not conform with the provisions of this constitution, the candidate is liable to suspension from the exercise of the orders already received. Outside of this particular provision, the Holy Father is content to reiterate the sanctions of the Council of Trent, although graver penalties may be inflicted on either the ordaining prelate or the ordinand.[176] The legislation is subsequently approved by Innocent XIII,[177] Benedict XIII[178] and Benedict XIV.[179]

The Constitution *Apostolicae Sedis*[180] of Pius IX (1846-1878) lists among the suspensions *latae sententiae Summo Pontifici reservatae* that which is incurred for a year from the administration of orders by a bishop who has ordained his own subject without testimonial letters from the ordinary of any place where that subject has lived long enough to contract a canonical impediment. In this constitution there is no mention of a penalty for the one ordained. Hence the former provision in this respect lapses, and the recipient of orders is no longer forbidden the exercise of the order received.

This enactment of Pius IX has universal application, but with the permission of the Holy Office a suppletory oath may be substituted for the testimonial letters. When acting with such permission, the sanctions of the constitution are not incurred.[181]

Secular clerics living for more than four months in Rome incur a *latae sententiae suspensio reservata ad beneplacitum S.Sedis* if they receive ordination from anyone other than their proper bishop with-

[176] *Ibid.*, §§ 7-8.

[177] Const. *Apostolici ministerii*, 23 maii 1723, § 6—*Fontes*, n. 280.

[178] Const. *In supremo*, 23 sept. 1724, §§ 4, 28—*Fontes*, n. 283. Cf. Wernz, *Ius Decretalium*, II, nn. 42-4; Aguilar, *Institutiones Iuris Canonici* (Santo Domingo de la calgada, 1904), p. 61.

[179] Const. *Impositi Nobis*, 27 febr. 1747, § 11—*Fontes*, n. 376.

[180] 12 oct. 1869, § V, n. 3—*Fontes*, n. 552. Cf. Pennacchi († 1898), *Commentaria in Constitutionem Apostolicae Sedis* (2 vols. Romae, 1883), II, app. XLIV, 365-85; D'Annibale (1815-1892), *Constitutionem Apostolicae Sedis Commentarii* (ed. 4, Prati, 1894), n. 201; Téphany († after 1898), *Constitution Apostolicae Sedis Commentaire* (Tours, 1883), nn. 567-8; Santi (1830-1885), *Praelectiones*, lib. I, tit. 11, n. 40; Ojetti (1862-1932), *Synopsis Rerum Moralium et Iuris Pontificii* (ed. 3, Romae, 1912), n. 3957.

[181] S.C.C., *Urgellen.*, 26 ian. 1895—*Fontes*, n. 4293.

out a previous examination before the cardinal vicar of Rome. The same penalty is also incurred if they receive ordination from their own ordinary after being rejected in this examination. In both cases the ordaining bishop is suspended for a year from the use of the pontificals.[182]

HISTORICAL SUMMARY

In decretal law there is ample evidence of the desire of the Church that the recipients of orders be worthy of the vocation in which they are called. A two-fold examination helps to safeguard this ideal by a comprehensive investigation of the candidate whose qualifications are unknown. The bishop may conduct this enquiry either personally or through the employment of learned and prudent examiners. At the time of Innocent III the archdeacon is noted as such an examiner.

When necessary, the examination includes a consideration of the age, knowledge and character of the ordinand, but the examiners are not limited to these subjects. Failure to adhere to the law makes both examinee, when deceitful, and examiner, when negligent, liable to punishment.

In the period prior to the Council of Trent a need for reform is recognized. This is provided for in the Council by an explicit determination of the qualities of the candidate for orders. The primary responsibility for the investigation belongs to the proper bishop of the ordinand. However, in fulfilling his duty he may call others to his assistance.

In the course of time emphasis is placed on one or another aspect of the legislation. Thus, there is a determination of the conditions under which testimonial letters are required of other bishops, pastors, and religious superiors. Particular care is exercised when impediments may have been contracted. In practice, the second ex-

---

[182] Pius IX, const. *Apostolicae Sedis,* 12 oct. 1869, § V, n. 7—*Fontes,* n. 552. Cf. Pennacchi, *op. cit.,* app. XLVIII, 417-29; D'Annibale, *op. cit.,* nn. 208-11 Téphany, *op. cit.,* nn. 586-91; Ojetti, *op. cit.,* n. 2076.

amination tends to be restricted to an investigation of the knowledge of the aspirant.

Except for the temporary legislation of Sixtus V, the sanctions applicable for any violation of the law remain as determined by the Council of Trent. The only notable change prior to the Code of Canon Law is the omission from the Constitution *Apostolicae Sedis* of a penalty for the one who is ordained in defiance of the laws on the examination of ordinands.

PART TWO
CANONICAL COMMENTARY

CHAPTER III

ATTESTATIONS REQUIRED BY THE CANDIDATE FOR ORDERS

Article I. *Subject Requiring Various Attestations*

In the introductory part of canon 993 there is a general declaration designating those who are affected by the subsequent sections of this canon. These subjects are the *promovendi* or the candidates for advancement. It matters not that orders may already have been received. As long as the physical person is an aspirant to some order, he is included in the number of those comprehended by this first word of the canon. "*Promovendi*" is a general term applicable to all. In distinguishing it the nature of the candidate as a secular, as a religious governed by the law of seculars, or as a religious bound by the norms of canon 995, must be considered. In the present chapter it is only the first of these three categories, i.e., the seculars, who are treated. A subsequent chapter includes all the religious.

The seculars here referred to may be either laics or clerics.[1] In both there must be the intention of receiving one of the orders. For laymen it is the initial step that is contemplated, while the cleric is already the recipient of at least the first tonsure and expects to advance further by ordination.[2] In neither case is the candidate associated with a religious institute. Although clerics and laics may be

[1] Cf. McBride, *Incardination and Excardination of Seculars*, p. 308.

[2] Can. 108, § 1. Cf. Beste, *Introductio in Codicem* (St. John's Abbey: Collegeville, Minn., 1938), p. 165; Raus, *Institutiones Canonicae iuxta Novum Codicem Iuris* (ed. altera, Lugduni: Vitte, 1931), p. 89; Blat, *Commentarium Textus Codicis Iuris Canonici* (5 vols. in 6, Romae, 1921-1927), II, 55.

religious,[3] the only ordinands now considered are those who are not religious.

The reason why these subjects are designated as *promovendi* is traceable to their desire to be ordained. As long as any of the orders, from the first tonsure to the priesthood, is sought, this canon is applicable. There is nothing in the nature of the matter or the wording of the canon to exclude any of the orders.[4] Consequently, ordination is here understood in the proper legal signification of the term[5] and includes not only the major and relatively minor orders, properly so-called,[6] but also the first tonsure.[7]

By this introductory clause it is the candidate who is enjoined to produce the attestation and testimonial letters listed in the subdivisions of canon 993. The word employed by the legislator is *afferant,* indicating that the ordinand himself has the obligation of obtaining the various documents.[8] This is in accord with the necessity which rests upon the candidate to show his worthiness to receive orders. However, there is lacking an explicit designation of the party to whom the various attestations are conveyed. The composition of this canon indicates the content and source of the required testimonials but it is necessary to look elsewhere to ascertain the authority to whom they are to be submitted.

Wernz-Vidal,[9] Moeder,[10] and McBride[11] teach that the one to whom these documents are sent is the ordinary with the right to ordain[12] or to grant dimissorial letters.[13] This opinion is in accord with canon 968, § 1, which demands for lawfulness that the candidate be, in the judgment of his proper ordinary, endowed with the

[3] Can. 107.

[4] Cf. Can. 950.

[5] Can. 18.

[6] Can. 949.

[7] Can. 950.

[8] Cf. Many, *De Sacra Ordinatione,* p. 323.

[9] *Ius Canonicum* (7 toms. in 9 vols., Romae: Apud Aedes Universitatis Gregorianae, 1923-1938), tom. IV, *De Rebus,* Pars I, 361.

[10] *The Proper Bishop for Ordination and Dimissorial Letters,* p. 91.

[11] *Incardination and Excardination of Seculars,* p. 535.

[12] Cf. cans. 956, 957, 959.

[13] Cf. can. 958.

qualities requisite for ordination. In forming his judgment this proper ordinary must have the attestations which are his guideposts in the matter. This is also true even when the proper bishop is not the actual minister of ordination. He still is obliged to pass on the worthiness of the aspirant, and his conclusion in this regard is expressed in the dimissorial he issues.[14]

Article II. *Attestations Relative to the Reception of the Sacraments*

A. *Baptism*

Various canons in the title of the Code treating of the sacrament of orders employ the term *"testimonium"* to designate an attestation to a particular fact issued by one competent to certify the existence of the fact.[15] This ability is not peculiar to an ordinary, but extends to such others as the rector of the seminary.[16] These testimonies, attestations or certificates are of such a nature as to be pertinent in other matters besides the reception of orders. Thus, a certificate of baptism is also necessary for the sacrament of matrimony.[17]

The first part of canon 993 clearly points to proof of baptism as being of primary importance in any consideration of the status of the ordinand. For a layman contemplating admission to the first tonsure, this is the fundamental requirement; for a cleric, this proof of baptism is presumed as already given prior to his entrance into the clerical state.

In speaking of the first tonsure the canon is referring to the medium of transition from the lay to the clerical state of life.[18] As a condition necessary for the validity of this change it is required that the candidate be baptized[19] by the pouring of true and natural

[14] Can. 960, § 1.

[15] Cf. cans. 960, §§ 1, 2, 3; 993, 1°, 2°, 3°.

[16] E.g., can. 993, 3°. Cf. Cappello, *Summa Iuris Canonici* (3 vols., Romae: Apud Aedes Universitatis Gregorianae, 1930-1936), II, n. 851.

[17] Can. 1021, § 1.

[18] Can. 108, § 1. Cf. S. Thomas Aquinas, *Summa Theologica* (ed. Faucher 4, Parisiis: Lethielleux, 1926), Suppl., q. XL, a. 2.

[19] Can. 968, § 1.

water while the prescribed words are pronounced.[20] It is this form of baptism, impressing a sacramental character,[21] and imparting the capacity to receive the other sacraments,[22] that is considered here. The baptisms of blood and desire are excluded.[23]

Assurance of the baptism of the candidate may be derived from the certificate he produces.[24] This is a public document[25] drawn from the baptismal register in the care of the pastor[26] or from the authentic copy of this register transmitted to the episcopal curia.[27]

The information available consists of the names of the person baptized, the minister of the sacrament, and of the parents and sponsors, together with the notation of the place and date of the baptism.[28] However, the certificate, having the same value as the register itself "fully proves only the fact of the baptism conferred upon the individual named, the date of the baptism, the identity of the godparents, and also that of the minister who conferred the sacrament. . . But the accessory information, such as that of the date

[20] Can. 737, § 1.

[21] Can. 732, § 1.

[22] Can. 737, § 1.

[23] Cf. Cappello, *Tractatus Canonico-Moralis de Sacramentis* (4 vols., Romae: Marietti, 1927-1932), II, Pars III, *De Sacra Ordinatione,* 309; Wernz-Vidal, *Ius Canonicum,* tom. IV, *De Rebus,* Pars I, 261; Blat, *Commentarium,* III, *De Sacramentis,* 21; Ayrinhac, *Legislation on the Sacraments in the New Code of Canon Law* (New York: Longmans, Green, 1928), p. 324; Coronata, *Institutiones Iuris Canonici* (5 vols., Taurini: Marietti, 1928-1936), I, 118.

[24] Can. 1816. Cf. Noval, *Commentarium Codicis Iuris Canonici,* Lib. IV, *De Processibus,* Pars I, *De Iudiciis* (Augustae Taurinorum, 1920), p. 370.

[25] Can. 1813, § 1, 4°. Cf. Vermeersch-Creusen, *Epitome Iuris Canonici* (3 vols., ed. 5, Mechliniae: Dessain, 1933-1936), III, 91; Chelodi, *Ius de Personis iuxta Codicem Iuris Canonici* (ed. altera a Bertagnolli recognita et aucta, Tridenti, 1927), p. 379.

[26] Can. 470, § 1.

[27] *Ibid.,* § 4. Cf.. can. 383, § 1; Louis, *Diocesan Archives,* The Catholic University of America Canon Law Studies, n. 137 (Washington, D. C.: The Catholic University of America Press, 1941), p. 49.

[28] Can. 777, § 1. Cf. O'Rourke, *Parish Registers,* The Catholic University of America Canon Law Studies, n. 88 (Washington, D. C.: The Catholic University of America, 1934), pp. 46-56; Fanfani, *De Iure Parochorum ad Normam Codicis Iuris Canonici (Taurini:* Marietti, 1924), p. 222.

of birth, of the qualities and conditions of the persons or of their domiciles, is not fully proved by the fact of its being recorded in such public registers."[29]

It is possible that there may be additions to the baptismal register noting the reception of confirmation,[30] the contraction of marriage,[31] a declaration of nullity,[32] the reception of the subdiaconate,[33] or the transaction of solemn profession.[34] There is indeed a presumption favoring the truth and reality of these recorded facts by the very reason of their being noted in the register,[35] but the register and the certificate dependent on it offer full proof only concerning the facts of baptism.[36]

To be acceptable as an authentic document[37] the certificate presented by the ordinand must be signed by the pastor or another competent public person, and it must also bear the impress of the parochial seal.[38]

The Code does not give a curate the power to issue such a certicate and his competence to do so must be derived from diocesan statutes, the authority of the ordinary, and the commission received

[29] Willett, *The Probative Value of Documents in Ecclesiastical Trials,* The Catholic University of America Canon Law Studies, n. 171 (Washington, D. C.: The Catholic University of America Press, 1942), p. 76.

[30] Can. 798.

[31] Can. 1103, § 2.

[32] Can. 1988.

[33] Can. 1011.

[34] Can. 576, § 2.

[35] Willett, *op. cit.,* p. 79.

[36] Noval, *De Iudiciis,* p. 370; Cocchi, *Commentarium in Codicem Iuris Canonici* (5 vols. in 8, Taurinorum Augustae: Marietti, 1925-1930), lib. IV, p. 292.

[37] Cf. can. 1813, § 1, 4°.

[38] Cf. cans. 470, § 4; 1813, § 4, 4°; Noval, *op. cit.,* p. 368; Blat, *Commentarium,* V, 328; Ayrinhac, *Constitution of the Church in the New Code of Canon Law* (New York; Benziger, 1925), p. 350; De Meester, *Juris Canonici et Juris Canonico—Civilis Compendium* (ed. nova, 3 vols. in 4, Brugis: Sumptibus et Typis Societatis Sancti Augustini, 1921-1928), II, 322; O'Rourke, *Parish Registers,* p. 13; Wanemacher, *Canonical Evidence in Marriage Cases* (Philadelphia: Dolphin Press, 1935), p. 209.

from the pastor.[39] In itself this particular task pertains to an ecclesiastical notary[40] exercising authority in the matters for which he is constituted.[41] Universal custom attributes this notarial power to the pastor;[42] others must not only be delegated for this purpose, but prior to such delegation are not even allowed access to the records.[43]

When a certificate is unobtainable, other provisions of the Code indicate how the desired proof may be supplied. Generally, as long as the interests of a third party are not involved, one reliable witness is sufficient to prove the fact. If there is question of a baptism received in adult age, the oath of the party is proof enough.[44]

Is canon 779 applicable here in that the baptism of the candidate may be considered as proved by the oath of one witness or of the ordinand himself? Since the word *"praeiudicium"* of this canon is understood in its historical origins as referring to a contentious case it seems that, strictly speaking, canon 779 may be invoked. However, whether the Holy See will admit proof of a fact, relatively so important in its consequences, by means of such an oath is not altogether clear. In the case where the presumptions arising from Catholic parentage or education[45] cannot be invoked it would seem pre-

[39] Can. 476, § 6: Eius iura et obligationes ex statutis dioecesanis, ex litteris Ordinarii et ex ipsius parochi commissione desumantur. . . Cf. De Meester, *op. cit.*, II, 347, nota 6; Waldron, *The Minister of Baptism*, The Catholic University of America Canon Law Studies, n. 170 (Washington, D. C.: The Catholic University of America Press, 1942), p. 172; Wanenmacher, *op. cit.*, p. 208.

[40] Can. 374, § 1, 3°.

[41] *Ibid.*, § 2.

[42] Cf. S.C.C., *Platien.*, 3 iul. 1909—*AAS*, I (1909), 657-8.

[43] Can. 470, § 4.

[44] Can. 779: Ad collatum baptismum comprobandum, si nemini fiat praeiudicium, satis est unus testis omni exceptione maior, vel ipsius baptizati iusiurandum, si ipse in adulta aetate baptismum receperit. Cf. Blat, *Commentarium*, III, *De Sacramentis*, 73; Bouuaert-Simenon, *Manuale Juris Canonici* (Vols. I, III, ed. 3, 1930; Vol. II, 1931, Gandae et Leodii: Apud Auctores in Seminariis Gandavensi et Leodiensi), II, 60; Sipos, *Enchiridion Iuris Canonici* (ed. altera, Pecs: Ex Typographia "Haladas R. T.," 1931), p. 436; Ayrinhac, *Legislation on the Sacramentas*, p. 61.

[45] Cf. c. 3, X, *de presbytero non baptizato*, III, 43—Innocentius III (1198-1216), *Veniens ad apostolicam*, 13 apr. 1206—Potthast, n. 2749; S.C. de Prop. Fide, instr., 30 sept. 1848—*Fontes*, n. 4825.

ferable to seek the guidance of the Holy See.. Such a procedure would be in harmony with the rather strict attitude of the Church as evident in the history of the legislation on this phase of the sacrament of orders.

Doubt concerning the absolute applicability of canon 779 begets the necessity of seeking other norms with which the problem may be resolved with certainty. One possibility is provided by an analogous application of the procedure followed in ecclesiastical trials. A qualified witness, such as the pastor who performs the ceremony, is capable of proving the fact.[46] The same is true of the oath of two or three persons of unquestioned knowledge and veracity and against whom circumstances of self interest do not militate.[47]

Inability to establish proof of the fact by one of the above methodrs is sufficient to generate prudent doubt concerning the reception of the sacraments. As a result, the candidate is baptized conditionally.[48]

The process here described for proof of baptism is certainly necessary when the reception of the sacrament by the ordinand lacks prior demonstration. In the majority of cases the aspirant is a seminarian in the stricter sense and because documentary proof of his baptism is furnished at the time of his entry in the seminary[49] reference to this only need be made when he becomes a candidate for orders. This document, with the others pertinent to orders, is kept in the diocesan curia.[50] Thus, when the Sacred Congregation of the Sacraments[51] instructs the responsible persons that an *attestatio* concerning the reception of baptism be appended to the formal petition of a candidate for ordination, reference need only be made to the proof submitted at the time of his entry in the seminary. It is this necessity of proving only once the fact of baptism that causes the legislator to distinguish in canon 933, 1°, between the first tonsure and the other orders.

---

46 Can. 1791, § 1: Unius testis depositio plenam fidem non facit, nisi sit testis qualificatus qui deponat de rebus ex officio gestis. Cf. can. 1757.

47 Can. 1791, § 2.

48 Can. 732, § 2.

49 Cf. cans. 1363, § 2; 972; Gasparri, *De Sacra Ordinatione*, n. 686.

50 Can. 1010, § 1.

51 Instr. *Quam ingens*, 27. dec. 1930, § 2, n. 2.—*AAS*, XXIII (1931), 122.

B. *Confirmation*

Besides responding to the fundamental requisite of baptism for the validity of ordination,[52] for the lawful reception of the first tonsure the candidate must also furnish proof of his confirmation.[53] For the establishing of this proof a certificate may be drawn from the parochial or curial records.[54] If these are unavailable, then a presumption for or against the fact of confirmation may be derived from the presence or absence of an annotation in the baptismal register.[55] Of course, other elements, such as the prevalence of negligence or ignorance, may strengthen or weaken the presumption concerning this fact.

It may be that the reception of this sacrament will be proved by one witness or the oath of the candidate.[56] Non-existence of confirmation affects only the supposed recipient and is not detrimental to those over whom the power of orders is exercised.

Since proof of confirmation is provided for entry in the seminary,[57] reference has only to be made to this in order to give an attestation suitable for the first tonsure. As with baptism, the conferring of the first tonsure obviates the need for proof of confirmation when other orders are given.

Should none of the methods described give proof of the confirmation of the ordinand, with the result that there is a prudent doubt concerning the fact, the sacrament is conferred conditionally.[58]

C. *Ordination*

After the bestowal of an order the names of those ordained and

[52] Can. 968, § 1.

[53] Can. 993, 1°. Cf. can. 974, § 1.

[54] Cf. cans. 470, §§ 1, 3; 798; 1813, § 1, 4°.

[55] Cf. Willett, *The Probative Value of Documents in Ecclesiastical Trials,* p. 79.

[56] Can. 800: Ad collatam confirmationem probandam, modo nemini fiat praeiudicium, satis est unus testis omni exceptione maior, vel ipsius confirmati iusiurandum, nisi confirmatus fuerit in infantili aetate. Cf. Bouuaert-Simenon, *Manuale,* II, 71.

[57] Can. 1363, § 2.

[58] Can. 732, § 2.

of the minister, and a record of the time and the place, are entered in the special book kept in the diocesan curia.[59] To each of the recipients there is given a certificate attesting to his ordination. If the ordaining prelate is someone other than the proper ordinary, the certificate is shown to the proper ordinary so that the fact may be registered in the special volume in the archives.[60]

When an attestation to the reception of the order immediately preceding the one now desired is required by canon 993, 1°, this is not to be understood in the strict sense that a certificate must be produced. If the proper ordinary is the minister of the prior ordination, or also if the candidate has previously presented his certificate of ordination, new proof need not be submitted. In both cases the proper ordinary has only to refer to his own diocesan record to confirm the fact.

Due to loss or destruction, it may happen that a certificate or the records are unavailable. To cover this contingency there is no express provision in the Code. Only two of the authors give the point any consideration.

Cappello wavers in his attitude. In an early work[61] he invokes the analogy of law to the extent of drawing a perfect parallel with baptism and confirmation when a similar case arises for these two sacraments. Thus, the testimony of a reliable witness or the oath of the candidate himself is sufficient to establish the fact of ordination. However, part of this teaching is implicitly retracted by Cappello in a later work[62] where there is omitted any mention of the ad-

[59] Can. 1010, § 1.

[60] *Ibid.*, § 2: Singulis ordinatis detur authenticum ordinationis receptae testimonium; qui, si ab Episcopo extraneo cum litteris dimissoriis promoti fuerint, illud proprio Ordinario exhibeant pro ordinationis adnotatione in speciali libro in archivo servando.

[61] Cappello, *Summa Iuris Canonici,* n. 860: Ad collatam ordinationem probandam, si forte documenta archivi combusta aut amissa fuerint, satis est ex analogia legis (can. 779 et 800. . .) unus testis, omni exceptione maior (dummodo praeiudicium nemini fiat), v.g. Episcopus ordinans, cancellarius episcopalis, caeremoniarius etc., vel ipsius ordinati iusiurandum.

[62] Cappello, *De Sacramentis,* II, Pars III, 535: Ad collatam ordinationem probandam, si forte documenta archivi combusta aut amissa fuerint, satis est ex analogia legis (can. 779 et 800) unus testis, omni exceptione maior (dummodo praeiudicio nemini fiat), v.g. Episcopus, parochus, cancellarius episcopalis, etc.

missibility of an oath by the ordinand.

Wernz-Vidal[63] make no attempt to draw an analogy with baptism and confirmation. Their opinion is based on pre-Code legislation and thus admits of proof solely by witnesses. An oath by the candidate is expressly rejected as insufficient.

Since Cappello does not mention his change of mind, no evaluation of his reasoning is possible. On the other hand, Wernz-Vidal supply the omission by the same reference to the Decretals of Gregory IX as is found in the *fontes* for canon 993,[64] a reply of the Holy Office,[65] and the Synod of Alexandria held in 1898.[66]

In the Decretals, St. Raymond included the answer to a question proposed to Innocent III (1198-1216) by the patriarch of Constantinople. The inquiry concerned the status of clerics who lacked letters, but who were willing to swear to the fact of their ordination. The Holy Father, in reply, instructed the patriarch that he was neither to receive these strangers nor to promote them to major orders unless the patriarch was satisfied with their canonical ordination by suitable arguments. This mode of procedure was particularly pertinent as long as the candidates' approved manner of life was still unrecognized.

The tenor of this letter conformed to the general attitude toward *ignoti* as explained in the historical part of this work.[67] Something of this same attitude continues on into the present legislation. An attestation to ordination is required, but no specific provisions are made for the manner of proof in accord with which this requirement must be met. Since identity with the old law is presumed,[68]

[63] *Ius Canonicum,* tom. IV, Pars I, 387: Ordinationis probatio praeter litteras etiam per testes fieri potest, sed solum iuramentum ordinatorum de ordinatione canonice recepta sufficiens argumentum non est.

[64] C. 2, X, *de clericis peregrinis,* I, 22—Innocentius III, *Inter quatuor,* aug. 1206—Potthast, n. 2860.

[65] 9 apr. 1704—*Collectanea S. Congregationis de Propaganda Fide seu Decreta, Instructiones, Rescripta pro Apostolicis Missionibus ex Tabulario eiusdem Sacrae Congregationis Deprompta* (Romae, 1893), n. 1170.

[66] Wernz-Vidal, *op. cit.,* p. 387.

[67] Cf. *supra,* chap. I, art. I.

[68] Can. 6, 4°.

the oath of the candidate is now considered insufficient, just as it was prior to the Code.

The declaration of the Holy Office noted by Wernz-Vidal concerned priests and deacons converted from schism. However, it had an indirect application to the matter now being considered. The fact of ordination was supposed as proved by other means while the word of the party involved was accepted concerning the manner of ordaining. There was established the procedure which was to be followed when the ordination was of either certain or doubtful validity, and when it was unquestionably null.

These citations are less than apodictic, but they are indicative of a persevering attitude of the Church in the matter of ordination. In keeping with this it is suggested that proof of the reception of orders be sought from a qualified or at least two other witnesses of unquestioned integrity.[69]

Should proof of ordination by any of the methods indicated above be unobtainable, the order in question is conferred conditionally.[70] Inability to furnish proof normally is sufficient reason to cause prudent doubt concerning the reception of the orders.[71]

It is noteworthy that there is additional reason for obtaining proof of ordination in the case of a candidate receiving some orders as an Oriental and then securing permission from the Apostolic See to undertake higher orders in the Latin rite.[72] In such a case there must be a fully reliable determination not only of the last but also of the other orders conferred, for the purpose that there may be supplied in the Latin rite the orders which were not conferred in the Oriental rite.[73] This procedure is necessary only once. In subsequent ordinations the presumption stands that the omissions have been supplied, just as after the first tonsure baptism and confirma-

[69] Cf. can. 1791.

[70] Can. 732, § 2.

[71] Note: Due to the ravages of the war currently raging, many records undoubtedly will be destroyed. Because of this, suspicion of a candidate unable to prove his ordination should be notably diminished.

[72] Cf. can. 1004.

[73] Cf. can. 1004; Benedictus XIV, const. *Etsi pastoralis,* 26 maii 1742, § VII, n. VII—*Fontes,* n. 328; Beste, *Introductio,* p. 540.

tion are abidingly honored as established facts. If there is question of an Oriental baptized in Russia, a presumption in favor of his reception of the subdiaconate may be established from the notation of its reception sent to the Sacred Congregation for the Oriental Church.[74]

Article III. *Supplementary Attestations*

A. *Studies*

Besides the reception of the sacraments there are various other requirements to which there must be an attestation. The first of these pertains to the studies completed for each order according to the norms of canon 976.[75] The relationship between studies and ordination, as indicated by this canon, is to serve as the determinant of the attestation required by canon 993, 2°. The relationship is expressed in the first two paragraphs of canon 976. The third section is excluded from consideration by the fact that the reference of canon 993, 2°, is *ad normam* and not *secundum can. 976.* Consequently, a candidate studying under the dispensation provided by canon 972[76] may furnish a testimony to his studies even though they are undertaken outside the schools referred to by canon 976, § 3. It is for this same reason that no attestation to studies is required for the minor orders. Canon 976 determines no stated period in the course of theology for their reception.

First tonsure demands that the candidate have begun the formal course in theology. This course does not extend to such subjects as

[74] Cf. *AAS,* XX (1928), 260. Note: In a particular case other attestations may be needed, e.g., if the candidate has married, there must be proof of the death of the wife, of the dispensation which was granted for a ratified but unconsummated union, of the declaration of nullity, or of the permission granted by the Holy See to receive orders. Cf. Cappello, *De Sacramentis,* II, Pars III, 488, 499.

[75] Can. 993, 2°: Testimonium de peractis studiis, pro singulis ordinibus, ad normam can. 976, requisitis.

[76] § 1: Curandum ut ad sacros ordines adspirantes inde a teneris annis in Seminario recipiantur; sed omnes ibidem commorari tenentur saltem per integrum sacrae theologiae curriculum, nisi Ordinarius in casibus particularibus, gravi de causa, onerata eius conscientia, dispensaverit.

are of a theological nature but are included in philosophical studies.[77]

In attempting to determine precisely what constitutes the inception of the course in theology, the authors give varying interpretations of canon 976, § 1. The stricter view requires that the conferring of orders be deferred until the lectures actually commence. However, the milder understanding of Cappello[78] and Bolduc[79] is admissible. Consequently, an attestation to the commencement of the study of theology may be obtained by the ordinand as soon as he has registered. This start of theological studies is the only fact to be verified since the canon demands no more. It is supposed that the authorities of the seminary or the priest to whose care the candidate is given[80] are sure of the presence of the fundamental scholastic requirements before allowing the candidate to commence the study of theology.[81]

As long as the candidate is of age[82] and a year has elapsed since the reception of the last minor orders,[83] he may be ordained as a subdeacon at the end of the third year of his course in theology.[84] The incidence of Easter, Pentecost or the completion of two-thirds of the third year are commonly accepted as satisfying this demand.[85]

[77] Cf. can. 1365, §§ 2, 3; Augustine (1872-1944), *A Commentary on the New Code of Canon Law* (8 vols., St. Louis: Herder, 1918-1922), IV, 458; Ayrinhac, *Legislation on the Sacraments*, p. 339; Bolduc, *Les Études dans les Religions Cléricales,* The Catholic University of America Canon Law Studies, n. 149 (Washington, D. C.: The Catholic University of America Press, 1942), p. 117; Anon., "De studiis requisitis ante ordinationem," *Periodica,* XII (1923), (9).

[78] *De Sacramentis,* II, Pars III, 390.

[79] *Op. cit.,* p. 117.

[80] Can. 972, § 2. Cf. Beste, *Introductio,* p. 526.

[81] Cf. cans. 1364, 2°, 3°; 1365, § 1; Blat, *Commentarium,* III, *De Sacramentis,* 398.

[82] Can. 975.

[83] Can. 978, § 2.

[84] Can. 976, § 2: Firmo praescripto can. 975, subdiaconatus ne conferatur, nisi exeunte tertio cursus theologici anno; diaconatus, nisi incepto quarto anno; presbyteratus, nisi post medietatem eiusdem quarti anni.

[85] Cf. Blat, *loc. cit.;* Ayrinhac, *Legislation on the Sacraments,* p. 340; Bolduc, *Les Études dans les Religions Cléricales,* p. 117; Cappello, *De Sacramentis,* II, Pars III, 390; Anon., "De studiis requisitis ante ordinationem," *Periodica,* XII (1923), 10.

The advance to the diaconate may be considered with the commencement of the fourth year of theology. In the absence of an authentic determination to the contrary, the start of this year may be computed as for the first tonsure. Thus, the matriculation of the candidate suffices for an attestation to the fact that the fourth year has begun.

Finally, the testimony presented by the aspirant to the priesthood attests to his progress beyond the middle of the fourth year of the course. If the year is divided into semesters, the requirement is certainly satisfied by ordination at any time after the completion of the first semester.[86] In a continuous course the passage of five or even four and a half months is sufficient.

B. *Character*

In the Code of Canon Law there is ample indication of the mind of the legislator regarding the relationship between the various orders. First tonsure, the minor orders, subdiaconate and diaconate are considered as preliminaries to the priesthood, and the worthiness of the candidate is adjudicated principally in the light of his fitness to be ordained a priest.[87] That the students in seminaries may be endowed with the qualities necessary for the proper, holy and fruitful exercise of the priesthood, several instructions have been issued by the Holy See in recent years.[88] That of the Sacred Congregation of the Sacraments is particularly pertinent here. It is true that the norms indicated in this instruction need not be invoked in all cases, but their employment, to the extent possible and necessary, gives the bishop such information regarding the character of the ordinand as

[86] Cf. Cappello, *loc. cit.;* Hannan, "Ordinations at Christmas," *The Jurist* (Washington, D. C., 1941—), I (1941), 153-4.

[87] Can. 973, § 1: Prima tonsura et ordines illis tantum conferendi sunt, qui propositum habeant ascendendi ad presbyteratum et quos merito coniicere liceat aliquando dignos futuros esse presbyteros. Cf. Jorio, *Sacerdos Alter Christus: De Instructione pro Scrutinio ad Ordines Peragendo Commentarius* (Romae, 1933), p. 145.

[88] S.C. de Sacr., *Quam ingens,* 27 dec. 1930—*AAS,* XXIII (1931), 120-9; S.C. de Rel., *Quantum Religiones,* 1 dec. 1931—*AAS,* XXIV (1932), 74-81; S.C. pro Eccl. Orient., decr. 27 ian. 1940—*AAS,* XXXII (1940), 152-7. Cf. Pius XI, encyl. *De Sacerdotio Catholico,* 20 dec. 1935—*AAS,* XXVIII (1936), 5.

to enable him safely to proceed to ordain.[89] In certain cases some of the norms, e.g., those decreeing a special investigation by the bishop,[90] need not be followed but generally the specifications of the Instruction are to be applied.

The Sacred Congregation insists that the bishop or ordinary examining the character of the candidates reject those unsuited for the priesthood or devoid of a divine vocation in the very beginning and before admitting them to first tonsure and the minor orders.[91] Even though sacred orders are not conferred until the end of the course of studies, difficulties attendant upon the rejection of an unsuitable candidate increase with the approach of the end of this course.

Of paramount importance to the ordinary in making his judgment is the attestation of the rector of the seminary or of the priest to whom the candidate is entrusted outside the seminary.[92] So vital is this that it may provide reason for the rejection at the outset of the petition of the candidate for first tonsure and minor orders.[93]

The rector who is to make this report on the suitableness of the candidate is the priest, outstanding by reason of doctrine, virtue and prudence,[94] to whose care the discipline of the seminary is primarily

[89] *Quam ingens,* § 1, n. 4: Sed mens non est Sacrae Congregationi, ut omnes et singulae inquisitiones in singulis casibus absolute peragantur, cum non semel ex his nonnullae supervacaneae sint, aut non possibiles; sed ut ea colligantur, quae de moribus ordinandorum cognosci et explorata esse debent, antequam ad sacram Ordinationem tuto procedi possit.—*AAS,* XXIII (1931), 122. Cf. Larraona, "Animadversiones," *Apollinaris* (Romae, 1928—), IV (1931), 207; Cappello, *De Sacramentis,* II, Pars III, 368; Wernz-Vidal, *Ius Canonicum,* tom. IV, vol. I, 363; Jorio, *Commentarius,* p. 107.

[90] *Quam ingens,* § 1, n. 8—*AAS,* XXIII (1931), 124.

[91] Cf. Jorio, *op. cit.,* pp. 94-5.

[92] Canon 993, 3°: Testimonium rectoris Seminarii, aut sacerdotis cui candidatus extra Seminarium commendatus fuerit, de bonis eiusdem candidati moribus. Cf. can. 972.

[93] *Quam ingens,* § 2, n. 2—*AAS,* XXIII (1931), 121.

[94] Cf. can. 1360, § 1; Jorio, *Commentarius,* p. 84; Cox, *The Administration of Seminaries,* The Catholic University of America Canon Law Studies, n. 67 (Washington, D. C.: The Catholic University of America, 1931), pp. 76-7, 81-9.

confided.[95] If the ordinary in a particular case and for a grave cause dispenses the ordinand from attendance at a seminary, the information is sought of the pious and suitable priest entrusted with the care of the candidate.[96]

When the petition for ordination[97] is sent by the candidate to the bishop and there is no reason for rejecting it at once, the ordinary returns it to the rector with a mandate to investigate, in the name and by the authority of the bishop, the suitableness and qualities of the petitioner, as demonstrated during the period of his residence at the seminary.[98] In fact, someone other than the rector may be delegated for this purpose if the seminary lacks a moderator and someone else is in his place, or if the ordinary judges that another is better fitted to investigate in this case.[99]

After the delegation by the bishop, information is sought from the prefects and professors,[100] but not from the confessors.[101] Those to be heard are consulted, individually and as a group, on such signs of a vocation as piety, modesty, chastity, devotion to sacred functions, progress in study and character.[102] In diocesan seminaries the mem-

[95] Cf. can. 1358; *Litterae ab Excmo Delegato Apost. ad universos Civitatum Foed. Americae Sept. Ordinarios, nomine et auctoritate S.C. de Semin. et Stud. Univ. missis,* 26 mai. 1928—*Enchiridion Clericorum* (Romae: Typis Polyglottis Vaticanis, 1938), n. 1248.

[96] Cf. cans. 972; 1370.

[97] Cf. can. 992.

[98] *Quam ingens,* § 2, n. 4—*AAS,* XXIII (1931), 122.

[99] *Loc. cit.;* Larraona, "Animadversiones": Ut patet, mens S. Congregationis est ut Ordinarius non per sese sed per alios et generatim per Seminarii moderatores colligat notitias—*Apollinaris,* IV (1931), 208.

[100] Cf. can. 1369, § 1.

[101] Can. 1361, § 3: Quando agitur de alumno ad ordines admittendo vel e Seminario expellendo, nunquam confessariorum votum exquiratur. For the rôle of the confessor cf. Vermeersch, "Partes Confessarii in diudicanda virtute necessaria ad sacros ordines," *Periodica,* XVII (1928), 231*-41*; Jorio, *Commentarius,* pp. 155-9.

[102] *Quam ingens,* § 2, n. 5—*AAS,* XXIII (1931), 123. Cf. cans. 1357, § 3; 1367; Cappello, *De Sacramentis,* II, Pars, III, 384-6; Vromant, "De signis negativis vocationis sacerdotalis et religiosae," *Periodica,* XXII (1933), 187*-91*; Jorio, *Commentarius,* pp. 46-72, 96-9; Cox, *The Administration of Seminaries,* p. 78..

bers of the board of discipline[103] are also questioned when they, too, know the candidates. The information thus compiled is forwarded to the bishop. However, before sending it, the moderator of the seminary and the one taking his place add their own judgment of the character and sincerity of the aspirant.[104] This opinion is of particular importance inasmuch as the moderator is presumed to be in the best position to judge the candidates.[105]

To the instruction of the Sacred Congregation of the Sacraments there is appended an outline indicating the mode of investigation pursued outside the seminary. The procedure within the seminary is given only in the general terms expressed above. To supply for the lacuna and thus help the moderator in his discussions with the professors and prefects, Jorio[106] provides the following specimen:

1. Does the seminarian show all the positive signs of a vocation, viz., right intention, freedom from coercion, humility, charity, piety, spirit of labor, zeal, purity, knowledge of the obligations inherent in sacred orders, canonical requirements, freedom from irregularities?

2. Under what circumstances does he demonstrate rather negative signs of a vocation, viz., desire for an easier life, of attaining honors, of profit, of fleeing manual labor, of enjoying clerical privileges?

3. What is his attitude toward the common duties: those in the house and the chapel, services in the cathedral church, the monthly or annual periods of recollection?

4. Is he diligent in the practice of weekly confession, of frequent and even daily communion;[107] what start and progress has he

[103] Can. 1359.

[104] *Quam ingens*, § 2, n. 8—*AAS*, XXIII (1931), 124.

[105] *Ibid.*, n. 5—*AAS*, XXIII (1931), 123.

[106] *Commentarius*, pp. 117-9.

[107] Note: The nature of this inquiry on the reception of Holy Communion is to be considered in the light of the special instruction issued by the Sacred Congregation of the Sacraments on Dec. 8, 1938 (*Periodica*, XXVIII (1939), 317-24). The apparent conflict between this later instruction and *Quam ingens* is resolved by Lopez. He adverts to the fact that both emanate from the one source, that the attitude of the student in the seminary toward the Eucharist is

made in piety, modesty, soundness of character?

5. Does he willingly serve at the altar and does he do so with modesty and dignity; does he teach the rudiments of the faith to children?

6. Does he frequently and sincerely speak of spiritual matters?

7. How great is the devotion he manifests toward the Sacred Heart, Blessed Mother, St. Joseph, the apostles Peter and Paul and the other saints?

8. Does he love the rule of the seminary and fully observe it?

9. Are there any signs, in word or work, against faith, hope, charity?

10. In the matter of chastity, does he nurture particular friendships and, if so, in what way is this indicated?

11. When censured does the candidate graciously accept the admonition and amend?

13. What is his attitude toward superiors, equals and inferiors?

14. What is the nature of his conversation; does he frequently speak of women?

15. Does he love his parents or, to the contrary, despise them because they may be of a poor condition?

16. How does he act in adversity; is he patient; resigned to the will of God?

17. Of what nature is he: secretive, candid, fickle, obstinate, etc.?

18. Is his attitude toward his fellows marked by charity; is he quick to argue or inclined to quarrel; does he nourish rivalries or grudges?

19. Are the norms of Christian charity observed toward inferiors or servants?

20. In school is the candidate submissive, attentive, diligent,

of great importance as a positive sign of a vocation to the priesthood, that the special instruction has a much broader application than *Quam ingens,* that the subject, object and end of both instructions differ. Cf. "De inquisitione circa pietatem ordinandorum et de animi liberate in usu Communionis frequentis," *Periodica,* XXIX (1940), 302-7.

docile; does he make adequate progress; does praise cause him to swell with vanity?

21. Is he orderly in his person?

22. Does he show himself grateful to the bishop, his parents and superiors, and does he speak respectfully of them?

23. Is his letter-writing to his parents and externs becoming and controlled?

24. Is he modest in his gait and does he observe custody of the eyes?

25. Does he consort with trouble makers?

26. What is his attitude toward the property of others?

Considerations such as these make possible a judgment of the character of the ordinand and his aptitude for orders.

When the aspirant progresses to the point where the subdiaconate is contemplated, the results of the investigation made preparatory to the reception of the first tonsure and the minor orders are again consulted.[108] There is then a repetition of the method already described for examining the character of the ordinand. However, the scope of this investigation is limited. There is no need to inquire into what has already been established, unless new reasons arise to warrant such a procedure. The main concern of the examination for the subdiaconate is the character and moral qualities of the ordinand, as demonstrated by his life in the seminary, and his progress in study.[109]

Ordinarily, the two investigations, that for the first tonsure and the minor orders and that for the subdiaconate, suffice. Should new circumstances arise and cause doubt concerning the purpose or moral suitableness of the candidate for the diaconate or the priesthood, a new investigation is made. If it be learned that the ordinand lacks a vocation, the bishop refers the matter to the Holy See with a full explanation of the reasons for doubting the worthiness of the candidate.

108 *Quam ingens,* § 1, n. 5: Acta, quae in huiusmodi perscrutationibus conficiuntur, asservanda erunt sub secreto in Curiae tabulario.—*AAS,* XXIII (1931), 122.

109 *Quam ingens,* § 3, n. 1—*AAS,* XXIII (1931), 125.

It is obvious throughout this procedure that great weight is attached to the testimony of the rector of the seminary where the aspirant is a student. His attestation is also of value when an ordinand transfers from one to another seminary. If the candidate is dismissed from the first seminary, the superior[110] of that institution has a grave obligation to indicate the cause for dismissal and give a judgment on the character, natural ability and capacity for study displayed by the ordinand while under his supervision.[111] This information is provided at the time of the change and is kept in the diocesan curia with the other documents relative to ordination. When orders are conferred, this material is consulted and is considered under canon 993, 3°, as testimony of the rector of the first seminary. Certainly, the value of this information is indisputable when compared with the judgment passed on the candidate at the second seminary.

Does this same obligation exist when the student is not dismissed, but leaves either of his own accord or at the instigation of his bishop? It seems that the answer must be in the affirmative. Canon 993, 3°, speaks without qualification of *testimonium rectoris Seminarii*. Thus, if the candidate transfers before the reception of any order, there is to be an attestation as to his character for the while he resided in the first seminary. If he leaves after receiving the first tonsure, the results of the fundamental investigation are reviewed. There is no difficulty in doing this if the candidate is still a member of the diocese for which he studied in the first seminary. Reference has only to be made to the records kept in the diocesan curia in conformity with the directions of the Sacred Congregation of the Sacraments.[112]

If there is a change of dioceses the process of excardination and incardination is followed. This involves the concession of attestations pertaining to the origin, life, character and studies of the

110 Can. 1363, § 3, speaks of *superiores*, but this is a general term including the rector under whose authority the other moderators serve. Cf. cans. 1360, § 2; 1369, § 1.

111 Can. 1363, § 3. Cf. Blat, *Commentarium*, IV, *De Rebus*, 298.

112 *Quam ingens*, § 1, n. 5.—*AAS*, XXIII (1931), 122.

candidate.[113] A precise delineation of the meaning of these terms is provided by McBride:

> It follows . . . that the testimony the Bishop needs to incardinate lawfully is substantially the same as to ordain lawfully, namely: 1) The parentage and origin of the candidate *(de clerici natalibus)*, which would include not merely the bare facts of his date of birth and legitimacy but also his moral, cultural, and social background. Though it is presumed that the first ordaining Prelate verifies the necessary facts of the candidate's legitimacy as well as his reception of the sacraments of baptism and confirmation, nevertheless, it still remains the prerogative of any Bishop who is interested in incardinating a cleric to judge of the cleric's desirability from the standpoint of his family history. 2) His life *(de clerici . . . vita)*, which means his record for righteousness, goodness, or moral integrity, for it must be known whether or not he is enmeshed in any irregularity or canonical impediment, whether or not he spent all his time in the diocese *"a qua,"* and, if not, how long elsewhere, and what was his record for good conduct while away. 3) His character *(de clerici . . . moribus)*, by which is signified the traits, habits, etc., which reveal it, such as zeal or indifference, a spirit of sacrifice or one of selfishness, and the like. 4) His studies *(de clerici . . . studiis)*, i.e. his creditable completion of the prescribed course of studies for the order which he presently has and his mental ability to pursue the requisite higher studies with at least some promise of success.[114]

This information is obtained from the curia of the diocese from which the candidate departs, but it is upon the ordinary of the first

[113] Can. 117, 2°: Ex legitimo documento sibi constiterit de obtenta excardinatione, et habuerit praeterea a Curia dimittente, sub secreto, si opus sit, de clerici natalibus, vita, moribus ac studiis opportuna testimonia, maxime si agatur de incardinandis clericis diversae linguae et nationis; Ordinarius autem dimittens, graviter onerata eius conscientia, advigilare debet ut testimonia sint veritati conformia.

[114] *Incardination and Excardination of Seculars*, pp. 535-6.

diocese that the ultimate and grave responsibility rests for the truthfulness of the various attestations. He, in turn, is dependent upon others, particularly the rector of the seminary, for the material submitted to the incardinating bishop. In the United States there is express provision for this. Both the Second (1866)[115] and Third (1884)[116] Plenary Councils of Baltimore decreed that a student transferring from one to another seminary must have letters from the superior of the seminary which he had left. As Hannan[117] points out, this legislation is *praeter Codicem* and is still in force.

[115] Tit. III, *De Personis Ecclesiasticis,* cap. VII, *De seminariis ecclesiasticis constituendis et ordinandis,* n. 180—*Acta et Decreta,* p. 110.

[116] Tit. V, *De Clericorum Educatione et Instructione,* cap. II, *De seminariis majoribus,* n. 176—*Acta et Decreta,* p. 90.

[117] "Ex-Seminarian and Novice," *The Jurist,* II (1942), 382.

CHAPTER IV

TESTIMONIAL LETTERS REQUIRED BY THE CANDIDATE FOR ORDERS

Article I. *Nature of the Testimonial Letter*

A. *General Considerations*

In defining a testimonial letter authors agree that its content is concerned with the worthiness of a candidate for orders. In expressing this idea, Prümmer (1866-1931),[1] Aertnys (1828-1915) Damen,[2] Bevilacqua,[3] Antonius a Sancto Joseph,[4] Ferreres (1861-1936),[5] Many († 1922),[6] Moeder[7] and Marc (1831-1887)-Gestermann[8] are satisfied with a more or less general statement that a testimonial letter gives assurance that the candidate is suitable for ordination. Wernz (1842-1914)-Vidal (1867-1938),[9] Blat,[10] Bouuaert-Simenon,[11] Vermeersch (1858-1936)-Creusen,[12] Cappello,[13] and

[1] *Manuale Theologiae Moralis* (ed. 8, 3 vols., Friburgi Brisgoviae: Herder, 1935-1936), III, 428.

[2] *Theologia Moralis* (ed. 12, 2 vols., Taurinorum Augustae: Marietti, 1922), II, 400.

[3] *De Episcopi seu Ordinarii Iuribus ac Obligationibus* (Romae, 1921) p. 128.

[4] *Compendium Salmanticense* (ed. 8, 2 vols., Burgis: Tipographia "El Monte Carmelo," 1931), II, 397.

[5] *Compendium Theologiae Moralis* (ed. 15, 2 vols., Barcinone, 1932), II, 481.

[6] *De Sacra Ordinatione*, p. 308.

[7] *The Proper Bishop for Ordination and Dimissorial Letters,* p. 90.

[8] *Institutiones Morales Alphonsianae* (ed. 19, 2 vols., Lugduni: Typis Emmanuelis Vitte, 1933-1934), II, 439.

[9] *Ius Canonicum,* tom. IV, vol. I, p. 361.

[10] *Commentarium,* III, *De Sacramentis,* 456.

[11] *Manuale,* II, 190.

[12] *Epitome,* II, 182.

[13] *De Sacramentis,* II, Pars III, 500.

Raus[14] are substantially in agreement with this declaration. They are more precise in that they specify more fully the extent of the matter covered by a testimonial. In accord with this second group of authors, a testimonial is here understood to be a declaration made by competent authority that the ordinand is fit to be ordained in that he has the necessary qualities and is free from canonical impediments. Under this meaning are included the testimonials of a local ordinary, of the major religious superior and of the pastor or other priest delegated by the ordinary to investigate.[15]

The testimonial itself is an attestation given solely for the purpose of receiving orders. In this it is distinguished from such others as the testimonials necessary for entry in a religious institute.[16] Ordinarily it is in writing and is preserved in the diocesan archives with the other documents pertinent to ordination.[17] The formalities observed are those which are employed for a public document, i.e., the signature of the one issuing the testimonial, his seal, and the notation of the date and place of issuance.

The mark of authenticity is impressed on a testimonial letter by the fact of its being granted by a public person acting in an official capacity. Prior to the Code the term *"Ordinarius"* was usually employed to designate those who were able to issue this letter to seculars. The actual extension of the term was disputed, but authors generally agreed that the bishop, the vicar-capitular, the abbot and the prelate *nullius* had the necessary power. They differed concerning the vicar-general, and the point of argument turned on the question of whether or not he needed a special mandate.[18]

The current legislation effects no change in the general designation of those who can grant the testimonial letter for a secular. The ordinary is vested with this power,[19] and since the vicar-general falls

[14] *Institutiones,* p. 92.

[15] Cf. cans. 993, 4°, 5°; 994; 1000, § 1.

[16] Cans. 544, §§ 2, 3, 4; 545, §§ 1, 4.

[17] Cf. can. 1010, § 1.

[18] Cf. Many, *De Sacra Ordinatione,* p. 319; Gasparri, *De Sacra Ordinatione,* n. 710.

[19] Cf. cans. 993, 4°; 994, §§ 2, 3; 198.

under this classification his status is no longer a matter for controversy. He requires a special mandate to issue a dimissorial letter,[20] but it is nowhere indicated in the Code that this is also true in the case of the testimonial. Between the two types of letters there is a great difference. The former is the medium by which there is conceded the faculty of ordaining the subject of another; the latter only vouches, as known to the one granting it, for the fitness and freedom of the aspirant from canonical impediments. Moreover, the issuance of a testimonial is not properly an act of jurisdiction, even in the broad sense in which the concession of a dimissorial is.[21]

This designation of the local ordinary is further particularized by the residence of the candidate in a place for such a length of time that a canonical impediment may be contracted.[22] The exclusive basis for this letter is a stay in a place for a determined period of time. This is a change in the law. Formerly the fundamental norms, as established in the Constitutions *Speculatores*[23] and *Apostolicae Sedis*,[24] emphasized the necessity of a testimonial from the ordinaries of the places of origin and also of other places where residence was so prolonged that an impediment could have been incurred. In the present law there is no reference to either domicile or origin.

The testimonial letter is of such a nature that, unless the conditions of canon 994, § 3 are fulfilled, it is required only once to cover the period of residence specified in the law.[25] Certainly there is no need for a local ordinary to attest over and over again, before the reception of each order, that the candidate is, as far as he knows, worthy. Once obtained, the testimonial is valid for all orders unless some circumstance begets need for a new letter.[26]

[20] Can. 958, § 1, 2°.

[21] Cf. can. 958; Gasparri, *op. cit.*, n. 708; Many, *op. cit.*, p. 154; Cappello, *De Sacramentis*, II, Pars III, 501.

[22] Can. 993, 4°: Testimoniales litteras Ordinarii loci in quo promovendus tantum temporis moratus est ut canonicum impedimentum contrahere ibi potuerit.

[23] Innocentius XII, 4 nov. 1694—*Fontes*, n. 258.

[24] Pius IX, 12 oct. 1869—*Fontes*, n. 552.

[25] Cf. can. 994, § 1.

[26] Cf. cans. 960, § 2; 994, § 3.

B. *Relation to Canonical Impediments*

Although the position of the vicar-general is clarified, the difficulty of the old law[27] regarding the meaning of the term *"canonicum impedimentum"* continues in the Code. The law merely states that testimonial letters are obtained from those ordinaries in whose territory the candidate resides long enough to contract such an impediment.[28] This procedure is in accord with the general attempt to ascertain the fitness of the ordinand. The particular provision is designed at least to uncover an obstacle, if one exists, to the reception of orders.

There is no doubt that the canonical impediment referred to in canon 993, 4°, includes the irregularities and simple impediments listed in canons 984, 985 and 987. The candidate stigmatized with any of these may not lawfully be ordained.[29]

The irregularities are perpetual and are not destroyed by the passage of time.[30] Thus, if an ordinand spends three or six months in a diocese, according to the prescription of canon 994, § 1, years before his contemplated ascent to orders, there remains an obligation to obtain a testimonial from the ordinary of that place. This ordinary may possibly testify either that the aspirant lacks some necessary quality[31] or is guilty of a delict[32] committed under the conditions delineated in canon 986.

Simple impediments[33] also characterize the candidate as unworthy, but they are only temporary and lack such a basis as the sin or defect on which an irregularity is founded. If the ordinand is or was burdened by a simple impediment, the ordinary of the place can testify simply as to his present status.

The local ordinary who restricts his testimony to a consideration of these irregularities and simple impediments is attempting to

[27] Cf. S.C.C., *Pragen.*, 25 iun. 1904—*Fontes,* n. 4318; Many, *De Sacra Ordinatione,* pp. 316-8.

[28] Cf. cans. 993, 4°; 994.

[29] Can. 968, § 1.

[30] Cf. cans. 983-985.

[31] Can. 984.

[32] Can. 985.

[33] Can. 987.

observe the law in its most limited acceptation. Should he go beyond this and testify to other aspects of the ordinand relative to his worthiness to be ordained?

It seems that *canonicum impedimentum* is understood in a sense more comprehensive than that indicated above. The foundation for this opinion is the general intention that only the worthy be advanced to orders. The law provides for this with the demands that (a) only those who are endowed with the required qualities and are free of any irregularity or other impediment be ordained;[34] (b) there be promise, even for the first tonsure, that the candidate will be worthy to be a priest;[35] (c) for sacred orders the bishop be morally certain of the suitableness of the aspirant.[36]

Not only these requirements, as specified in the canons, but the very idea behind the establishment of a definite list of canonical impediments argues for an extensive understanding of *canonicum impedimentum*. In an impediment the main factor concerns what is incongruous in relation to the clerical state. Some things are expressly enumerated in the law as falling in this category. There are others of a similar nature, but not mentioned so explicitly, e.g., an immoral life while in a particular place, even though the conduct was not of such a nature as to render the party infamous. It seems that data on these latter considerations should also be included in a testimonial letter. It is in this wider understanding of the term that there is conformity between the doctrine of the present Code and the common opinion of the authors cited at the beginning of this chapter.[37]

Article II. *Determinant of Time for a Testimonial Letter*

A. *Basic Notions*

The length of time in a place, making the contracting of a canonical impediment likely, is determined as ordinarily being three

[34] Can. 968, § 1.
[35] Can. 973, § 1.
[36] *Ibid.*, § 3.
[37] Chap. IV, art. I. Cf. Cappello, *De Sacramentis*, II, Pars III, 503.

months for a soldier and six months after puberty for others.[38]

In computing these periods of three months and a half year, canon 34, § 3, 3°, is invoked, and not canon 34, § 2, as Blat[39] asserts. The reckoning for a testimonial is implicitly determined by the time of entry into a place.[40] The passage of three or six months as computed in this manner, with the first day not counted and the period concluding with the end of the last day bearing the same date, establishes an obligation to procure a testimonial letter. However, there is no need to wait until the completion of the designated period. "There is a more or less accurate computation which at least approximates the reality of the truly physical reckoning of time."[41] If there is a reasonable cause, it is permissible to ask for an attestation for a space shorter than that determined in the canon.

This interpretation is supported by the acceptance of such a mode of moral computation prior to the Code[42] and by the wording of canon 994, § 1.[43] There is the use of the word *"regulariter,"* indicating that the specified times are by no means absolute norms, but rather the ordinary durations for which the precaution of a testimonial is taken. This is further confirmed by the last half of the same paragraph, which allows the ordaining bishop to require of the aspirant a letter for an even shorter period, or also for a period antedating the ordinand's age of puberty. The three months and the half year are set down as definite periods for which an official attestation must be obtained, but this is not meant to be a restriction hampering

[38] Can. 994, § 1: Tempus quo promovendus potuit canonicum impedimentum contrahere est, regulariter, pro militibus trimestre, pro aliis semestre post pubertatem; sed Episcopus ordinans pro sua prudentia exigere potest litteras testimoniales etiam ob brevius commorationis tempus, et ob tempus quoque quod pubertatem antecessit.

[39] *Commentarium*, III, *De Sacramentis*, 459.

[40] Cf. Dubé, *The General Principles for the Reckoning of Time in Canon Law*, The Catholic University of America Canon Law Studies, n. 144 (Washington, D. C.: The Catholic University of America Press, 1941), pp. 203-5.

[41] *Ibid.*, p. 88.

[42] Cf. S.C.C., *Pragen.*, 25 iun. 1904—*Fontes*, n. 4318; *Urgellen.*, 26 ian. 1895—*Fontes*, n. 4293.

[43] Cf. Vermeersch-Creusen, *Epitome*, II, 182; Beste, *Introductio*, p. 537; Sipos, *Enchiridion*, p. 468.

the end of the law, which is the determination of the worthiness of the candidate relative to his reception of orders.

In investigating the ordinand the length of time for a testimonial is based on his status. Advertence to the military in a special manner, as distinguished from others, is not a feature introduced by existing legislation. Pre-Code replies of the Sacred Congregation of the Council showed a special concern for clerics in military service because of the possibility that impediments might have been contracted.[44] For these clerics three months sufficed to produce an obligation to obtain a testimonial; for others, including soldiers who were not clerics, there was no express legislation. In the latter case six months were commonly accepted because of the practice of the Roman curia, the intention of the common law, and the teaching of the doctors.[45]

What interpretation is now to be placed on the phrase *"pro militibus?"* Wernz-Vidal,[46] Cappello,[47] Blat,[48] Vermeersch-Creusen[49] and Bouuaert-Simenon[50] understand it in a general sense. They repeat the wording of the Code without reference to the old law. Is this common usage of the doctors correct?

In general, the Code here canonizes the practice of the Sacred Congregation of the Council as accepted prior to the current legislation. In particular, the phrase under consideration is more general than the pre-Code expression *"pro clericis ordinandis jam militiae addictis."*[51] In this there is an expansion of the ambit of the law. The application to clerics in military service is indubitable. The inclusion of all soldiers is another indication of a progressively stricter attitude in the matter of assuring worthiness in the candidate.

Against the interpretation whereby the phrase *"pro militibus"*

[44] *Firmana,* 9 sept. 1893—*Fontes,* n. 4288; *Urgellen.,* 26 ian. 1895—*Fontes,* n. 4293; *Pragen.,* 25 iun. 1904—*Fontes,* n. 4318.

[45] S.C.C., *Urgellen.,* 26 ian. 1895—*Fontes,* n. 4293.

[46] *Ius Canonicum,* tom. IV, vol. I, p. 361.

[47] *De Sacramentis,* II, Pars III, 504.

[48] *Commentarium,* III, *De Sacranentis,* 459.

[49] *Epitome,* II, 181.

[50] *Manuale,* II, 190.

[51] S.C.C., *Urgellen.,* 26 ian. 1895—*Fontes,* n. 4293.

is applicable to all soldiers, and not merely to clerics in the armed forces, reference to the old law is of no avail. This results not only from the wording of the present canon, but also from the doubtful value of the declaration to which recourse must be had. The cited responses of the Sacred Congregation of the Council lack any sign of being issued with the approval of or after consultation with the Roman Pontiff.[52]

In this classification of soldiers there are included all those who are enlisted in the military service. The law is not restricted to any one branch of the service, but extends to both the army and the navy, together with their subsidiaries at the time of actual conflict.

For others than those who are of the military, an elapsed period of six months after puberty gives rise to a need for a testimonial letter. Since men are the only subjects of orders,[53] legal puberty is attained on the completion of the fourteenth year.[54] As the wording of the canon indicates, the phrase *"post pubertatem"* can in its reference be associated only with the words *"pro aliis,"* and not with the words *"pro militibus."* Thus, in the conceivable case of a boy in military service before his fourteenth birthday anniversary, the testimonial mentioned in canon 994, § 1, is required.

B. *Extension of Ordinary Determinations*

A bishop may ordain no one to sacred orders unless he is morally certain from positive canonical arguments of the worthiness of the ordinand.[55] The objective evidence generating this certitude may be based on the information received from the proper ordinary when this ordinary is not the actual ordaining prelate. A dimissorial letter of itself does not give this satisfaction, even though the attestations required by canons 993-1000 are at hand before it is issued.[56] Either a testimonial letter is also necessary, or there should be included in

[52] Cf. Many, *De Sacra Ordinatione,* p. 313; Schmidt, "The Juridic Value of the *Instructio,*" *The Jurist,* I (1941), 305.

[53] Can. 968, § 1.

[54] Can. 88, § 2.

[55] Can. 973, § 3.

[56] Can. 960, § 1.

the dimissorial a statement to the effect that the candidate is endowed with the requisite qualities. Depending on what other information he has, the ordaining bishop accepts this testimony as satisfactory or rejects it as inconclusive. If he has reason to doubt that the ordinand is free of canonical impediments, the bishop may demand a testimonial letter from those local ordinaries where the candidate has lived for less than three or six months, even though this residence antedated the candidate's age of puberty.[57]

This concession, whereby the ordaining bishop may request more than is ordinarily required, stresses the need for worthiness in the candidate for orders. If there is prudent reason for questioning this fitness, a more thorough investigation is possible. However, the mere passage of such a short period of time in a place does not of itself prompt the need of additional guarantees. The fact of residence can however be modified by a cause which in the estimation of the bishop, demands a further investigation. Otherwise the bishop could hardly be said to act prudently when he decides that the further investigation is indicated in the case.

Is this right of the ordaining bishop restricted to him, so that the proper ordinary may not invoke it under similar conditions? An affirmative answer to this question seems inimical to the proper ordinary and contrary to the general intention of the legislator. The proper ordinary has the fundamental obligation of judging the aspirant.[58] Over and above what he determines, there are other safeguards. These provide against possible negligence or ignorance on the part of the proper ordinary. However, they are supplementary to the customary inquiry. If the proper ordinary, when he is not the actual minister, prudently judges that a testimonial is required for a shorter period he may demand it.[59]

On the other hand, is there a need for a testimonial if there is moral certainty that the ordinand is unhampered by any canonical

[57] Can. 994, § 1.

[58] Cf. can. 968, § 1.

[59] Episcopus ordinans qui litteras testimoniales severius exigere potest, tam is est cuius auctoritate ordinationes fiunt, id est regulariter Ordinarius loci, quam ipse ordinans, qui depellendi suspicionem ab ordinando suo ius et officium habet.—Vermeersch-Creusen, *Epitome*, II, 182.

impediment? Are the prescriptions of canons 993, 4°, and 994, § 1, so rigid as to be inflexible in their application?

The key to this problem is provided by canon 21.[60] The laws made to safeguard against a common danger are still of obligation, even though in a particular case the danger is non-existent. The legislation now under consideration is of such a nature as to fall under this rule. The law is formulated for the purpose of gaining assurance that the ordinand has the requisite qualities and is free of canonical impediments. This is the very nature of a testimonial letter.[61] If the candidate is known to be burdened with an impediment, then there is no reason for seeking this testimonial, for the evidence already available marks the candidate as unsuitable for ordination. It is when he is thought to be fit that the extra step is taken, and that a testimonial is asked of those ordinaries in whose dioceses he lived long enough to make possible the contraction of an impediment. On receiving this letter and the other attestations, the judgment is made and moral certitude effected. In such a procedure there is nothing irrational or prejudicial.[62]

C. *Renewal of a Testimonial*

If, after obtaining a testimonial and before the actual ordination, the candidate again spends the length of time specified in canon 994, § 1, in the same territory, a new letter is to be procured from the ordinary of that place.[63] By this prescription a guarantee is provided against a change in the candidate. This has the same effect

[60] Leges latae ad praecavendum periculum generale, urgent, etiamsi in casu peculiari periculum non adsit.

[61] S.C.C., *Pragen.*, 25 iun. 1904: . . . scopus et tota vis legis in exigendis litteris testimonialibus in eo posita est, ne quis aliquo irretitus canonico impedimento temere ad S. Ordines admittatur, atque ut de candidati idoneitate Episcopus ordinans certior usque evadat.—*Fontes*, n. 4318.

[62] Cf. Vermeersch-Creusen, *Epitome*, I, 123; Cicognani, *Canon Law* (ed. 2, Philadelphia: Dolphin Press, 1935), pp. 627-8; Toso, *Ad Codicem Iuris Canonici Commentaria Minora* (5 vols., Romae: Marietti, 1921-1927), I, 66.

[63] Can. 994, § 3: Si post obtentas litteras testimoniales et ante peractam ordinationem, promovendus praedicto temporis spatio in eodem territorio rursus moratus sit, novae litterae testimoniales Ordinarii loci necessariae sunt.

as a pre-Code practice which deferred the forwarding of the testimonial until immediately prior to the ordination.[64]

As Blat[65] points out, the wording of the canon supposes an interruption in the stay of the candidate in a particular place. If the resumption of residence is so prolonged that it extends for three or six months, a new testimonial is necessary. The same is also true if the aspirant, after securing all the testimonials, goes to a new territory and remains there for the period set in the law.

There is a difficulty if the interruption occurs, for example, after a month and a half or four months of residence, depending on whether or not the ordinand is a soldier. Is a testimonial to be secured if the candidate returns to the same place and the complete period adds up to three or six months? The general norm of a moral computation may not always be clearly applicable in such a case. Consequently, it is suggested that a testimonial be obtained for a soldier if his stay totals three months within the period of a half year, or, for others, if their stay comprises six months within a twelvemonth.[66]

Special provision is made for the case when a bishop ordains in virtue of a dimissorial from the proper ordinary. As long as this letter is known to be genuine, orders may lawfully be conferred.[67] However, the norms of canon 994, § 3, are still applicable in this instance. When additional attestations are required by this canon, the bishop must have them before proceding to impose hands.[68]

[64] Cf. IV Provincial Council of Milan (1576), c. VII—Mansi, XXXIV A, 231.

[65] *Commentarium,* III, *De Sacramentis,* 460.

[66] S.C.C., *Pragen.,* 25 iun. 1904: Quae autem interruptio haberi debeat sufficiens, ut Episcopus Ordinans tuto se dispensare possit ob onere requirendi has litteras testimoniales, a priori decerni nequit, sed potius ex locorum personarumque circumstantiis melius diiudicabitur. Quidquid sit, videant Emi Patres, utrum ad omnia dubia hac de re in posterum praecavenda, tutius foret, si nulla habita interruptionis ratione, indiscriminatim huiusmodi litteras testimoniales exigendas decerneretur, dummodo trimestre intra dimidium annum et semestre tempus intra annum completum fuerit.—*Fontes,* n. 4318.

[67] Can. 962.

[68] Can. 960, § 2: Si post datas ab Ordinario litteras dimissorias nova testimonia necessaria sint ad normam can. 994, § 3, Episcopus alienus ne ordinet, antequam eadem receperit.

Moreover, should the three or six months be spent in the diocese of the ordaining bishop, this bishop is himself obliged to gather the necessary data.[69]

Article III. *Oath Supplying for a Testimonial*

A. *Basis for the Substitution*

If the local ordinary neither of himself nor through others knows enough to testify concerning the status of the candidate while in his territory, or if the ordinand wanders through so many dioceses that it is impossible or too difficult to gather all the required testimonials, the ordinary is to supply for the omission of these letters, at least by a suppletory oath offered by the candidate.[70]

This local ordinary includes those who are specified in canon 198, § 2. He is further determined as the one in whose territory the ordinand lingers long enough, according to the usual or exceptional provisions of canon 994, § 1, that an impediment may be contracted. Whether or not the candidate is burdened in this way is the material for the testimony of the local ordinary. To give this account he must know the aspirant either of himself or through others. The need for such knowledge clearly shows that the issuance of a testimonial is not to be a merely perfunctory matter. By reason of its relation to the sacrament of orders, it is of great importance.[71] The ordinary who concedes this letter as a formality, without an indica-

[69] Can. 960, § 3: Quod si promovendus tempus sufficiens ad contrahendum impedimentum ad normam mem. can. 994 transegerit in ipsa diocesi Episcopi ordinantis, hic testimonia directe colligat.

[70] Can. 994, § 2: Si loci Ordinarius neque per se neque per alios promovendum satis noverit, ut testari possit eum, tempore quo in suo territorio moratus est, nullum canonicum impedimentum contraxisse, aut si promovendus per tot dioceses vagatus sit ut impossibile vel nimis difficile evadat omnes litteras testimoniales exquirere, provideat Ordinarius saltem per iuramentum suppletorium a promovendo praestandum.

[71] Non enim leviter sunt testimoniales exarandae, quibus fides vi ss. canonum in re tanti momenti praestanda est.—Blat, *Commentarium,* III, *De Sacramentis,* 459.

tion of his ignorance or of the limited extent of his knowledge, fails in a serious obligation.[72]

It is readily understood that under present conditions the ordinary frequently knows little or nothing of the candidate, particularly if he is a transient. Under these circumstances a testimonial may not be issued. The defect may be remedied by consultation with others, e.g., with the former pastor of the ordinand. However, there is no need to limit this inquiry, as Sipos[73] seems to do, to this pastor. If it is expedient, others, trustworthy and able to testify concerning the character and life of the candidate, are interrogated.[74]

As a result of this procedure the local ordinary may obtain enough information to warrant a declaration regarding the worthiness of the one desirous of ordination. He then communicates with the proper ordinary and through the medium of a testimonial indicates whether or not the aspirant is free of canonical impediments. On the other hand, diligent investigation may uncover little or nothing. In this case the local ordinary discloses the limitation of his knowledge.

Besides a lack of knowledge, there is also the likelihood that the ordinand moves through so many places that it is impossible or, if not impossible, at least too difficult to obtain the letters ordinarily required. The number of these places is not restricted to those of domicile and quasi-domicile. The determinant is more temporal than local in that the dioceses are judged by the standards of canon 994, § 1. However, the mere fact of residence in a large number of places does not excuse from the obligation of securing testimonials. There must be the added element of impossibility or great difficulty. Thus a candidate who has lived in a number of dioceses in the United States does not labor under the same handicap as does the soldier whose address has varied from country to country. The particular case is judged, and the ordinary decides whether or not conditions make the procurement of the letters impossible or too difficult.

The basis for this impossibility or great difficulty is expressed in

[72] Cf. S.C.C., *Urgellen.*, 26 ian. 1895—*Fontes,* n. 4293.

[73] *Enchiridion,* p. 468.

[74] Cf. can. 1000, § 1.

the clause *"si promovendus per tot dioceses vagatus sit."* Does the use of this expression mean that a plurality of places must be involved? If the candidate lives in only one other diocese before coming to the place where he now is, are impossibility and great difficulty elements to be considered?

Since worthiness to be ordained is not computed according to a mathematical formula, it appears that the number of places involved is irrelevant. The fundamental norms remain the same whether one or a hundred dioceses are concerned. The application of this is clear when testimonials are procurable from one or more dioceses but not from others. There is an obligation to obtain what letters can be secured. If impossibiliity or great difficulty exists in one instance, the obligation ceases for that case, but not for others unmodified by these circumstances. Thus, an ordinand in the United States has to obtain letters from the other dioceses in this country or on this continent. If this same aspirant resided in a land with which normal communication no longer exists, the ordinary reasonably judges that a testimonial from this place is unobtainable, or that too great difficulty is entailed in an attempt to secure it. In any event the existence of an impossibility or of too great difficulty in a particular case does not constitute a general absolution from the law. They are circumstances to be considered as applicable to each testimonial, and not to all the letters as a unit.

B. *The Substitution*

Lack of knowledge and the impossibility or too great difficulty in obtaining testimonials make necessary another provision for proof of the worthiness of the candidate. This is furnished by the last part of canon 994, § 2, which decrees that the ordinary at least have the ordinand take a suppletory oath.

The admissibility of such an oath under certain conditions is the continuation of a practice antedating the Code. There is this important change: no longer is it necessary to have recourse to the Holy See in an individual case or for faculties for a determined period.[75]

[75] Cf. S.C.S. Off., 27 apr. 1888—*AKKR*, LXXV (1895), 128; S.C.C., *Urgellen.*, 26 ian. 1895.—*Fontes*, n. 4293.

The common law now permits the invocation of the name of God on the part of the candidate that the ordinary may be assured that the aspirant is not the subject of a canonical impediment contracted in a particular place. In taking this oath the ordinand must fulfill the requisite conditions of truth, judgment and justice.[76] "*Truth* demands that the oath-taker testify to the truth, which he knows and as he knows it . . . *Judgment* requires sincere consideration of the reason for the taking of the oath. . . *Justice* . . . the affirmation or negation which the oath-taker wishes to corroborate must be lawful."[77]

This manner of procedure is analogous to that employed in a trial when a litigant is permitted to swear to his religious status.[78] As employed here, this oath takes the place of other proof.[79] It is subsidiary and invoked in a case of necessity.[80] In this instance one or the other testimonial is missing. The preferable course is to obtain all the letters, but since this cannot be done, the defect is supplied by the oath. The legislator demands this, but, as the use of *saltem* indicates, other forms of proof are not thereby excluded.[81]

Blat[82] and Cappello[83] declare that the proper ordinary, as the recipient of the testimonials, is to request the oath. Cappello adds that the oath is offered before the local ordinary or his delegate. Vermeersch-Creusen[84] concur in this opinion to the extent of restricting this right exclusively to the local ordinary. All are agreed that the

[76] Can. 1316, § 1: Iusiurandum, idest invocatio Nominis divini in testem veritatis, praestari nequit, nisi in veritate, in iudicio et in iustitia.

[77] Moriarity, *Oaths in Ecclesiastical Courts,* The Catholic University of America Canon Law Studies, n. 110 (Washington, D. C.: The Catholic University of America, 1935), p. 2.

[78] Can. 1830, § 1.

[79] Vox "saltem" aperte significat alias probationes et informationes minime excludi, imo desiderari, adeo ut nonnisi, illis deficientibus, locus sit iuramento suppletorio.—Cappello, *De Sacramentis,* II, Pars III, 505.

[80] Cf. can. 1829; Noval, *De Processibus,* p. 379; Wanenmacher, *Canonical Evidence in Marriage Cases,* pp. 365-6.

[81] Cappello, *loc. cit.;* Blat, *Commentarium,* III, *De Sacramentis,* 460.

[82] *Loc. cit.,* 459.

[83] *Loc. cit.*

[84] *Epitome,* II, 182.

ordaining bishop, if not an ordinary, does not have this faculty.

Keene,[85] mistakenly contends that the major superior of an exempt clerical institute, as an ordinary for his own subjects, is capable of demanding the oath of canon 994, § 2. This author errs in failing to realize that canon 994 is not applicable to exempt religious. Being governed by canon 995, they have no need for a suppletory oath. Not being obliged to produce the testimonials in the first place, there is no need for the exempt to supply for the absence of the letters.

Should the candidate refuse to take this suppletory oath he becomes suspect. A lacuna persists in the knowledge of the proper ordinary, and hence he cannot judge that the ordinand has the required qualities until this gap is closed. This may be accomplished by obtaining the necessary testimonials or some other form of proof devised by the ordinary.

Article IV. *Testimonials within the Diocese*

A. *Announcement of Ordination*

1. *Obligation of the Pastor*

Prior to the conferring of the three sacred orders there is a public announcement of the names of the candidates in their parish church.[86] This proclamation is reserved to the pastor,[87] but another may be delegated to make the actual declaration. Ordinarily those assisting the pastor in the care of souls within his parish are given competence to perform this task. Delegation, however, need not be

[85] *Religious Ordinaries and Canon 198,* The Catholic University of America Canon Law Studies, n. 135 (Washington, D. C.: The Catholic University of America Press, 1942), p. 63.

[86] Can. 998, § 1: Nomina promovendorum ad singulos sacros ordines, exceptis religiosis a votis perpetuis sive solemnibus sive simplicibus, publice denuntientur in paroeciali cuiusque candidati ecclesia; sed Ordinarius pro sua prudentia potest tum ab hac publicatione dispensare ex iusta causa, tum praecipere ut in aliis quoque ecclesiis peragatur, tum publicationi substituere publicam ad valvas ecclesiae affixionem per aliquot dies, in quibus unus saltem dies festus comprehendatur.

[87] Can. 462, 4°.

restricted to them. Even one temporarily assisting on the day when the publication is made may be designated for this purpose. The very fact of assignment to the service at which the ordination is announced seems to constitute sufficient delegation. As authors[88] point out for the parallel case of marriage, a deacon is permitted to do this.[89]

2. *Circumstances of Publication*

In canon 998, § 1, there is no indication of the place for the publication other than that it be made in the parish church of the aspirant. Domicile, quasi-domicile and actual residence are not mentioned. Does this mean that the announcement is made in any one of a number of possible parish churches, or must it be made in all of them?

The Code employs the expression *"in paroeciali cuiusque candidati ecclesia."* Although the singular is used, this is not to be construed as implying a restriction to one church. To the contrary, it indicates a lack of distinction and an obligation incumbent on every pastor of the ordinand.[90] In the number of these pastors are included those of domicile, quasi-domicile, and legal domicile. The last named is of importance only when the candidate is a minor,[91] as may occur in the case of an aspirant to the subdiaconate.[92] If the candidate has only a diocesan domicile, the notification is given in the parish of actual residence. If he is a seminarian, the parish within whose limits the seminary is located is not included among those where the publication is to be made. The canon is referring to a parish church which is in some way proper to the candidate, for the

[88] E.g., Vlaming († 1935), *Praelectiones Iuris Matrimonii* (ed. 3, 2 vols., Bussum, 1919-1921), I, 133; Roberts, *The Banns of Marriage*, The Catholic University of America Canon Law Studies, n. 64 (Washington, D. C.: The Catholic University of America, 1931), p. 61.

[89] Cf. can. 1342, § 1.

[90] Bouuaert-Simenon, *Manuale*, II, 191; Vermeersch-Creusen, *Epitome*, II, 183.

[91] Cf. can. 88, § 1.

[92] Cf. can. 975.

seminary, in reference to the parish, enjoys extraterritoriality.[93]

Although the canon directly refers to the parish church of the ordinand, former pastors may be indirectly obliged to make the publication of the impending ordination. This occurs when an ordinary is asked to forward a testimonial according to the prescriptions of canon 994, § 1. To implement his own data, this local ordinary may seek information of others,[94] particularly of the former pastor of the candidate. Then this pastor, either of his own accord or at the instigation of the ordinary, announces the proposed ordination with the intent of uncovering possible impediments.

If he deems it prudent to do so, the ordinary has the power to command that the publication be made in other churches. He enjoys the prerogative of having the ordination announced in any church in his territory. There is no obligation to do this other than that engendered by circumstances pointing to such an announcement as a likely source of information on the aspirant. Blat[95] suggests that the publication be made in a parish where the candidate stays for as long as six months.

Wherever the notification is given, the name of the one seeking ordination is announced.[96] Over and above this, the very nature of the matter demands that the nexus between this name and a contemplated reception of sacred orders be made clear. The proclamation is fashioned in such a manner that there is no doubt concerning the party and his desire to receive this particular order. If an ordinand is known by a distinctive name in a place, that name should be used. Thus, if Vincent E. Smith is commonly known as Elwood Smith, this latter designation is employed in the publication. Moreover, it also should be understood that the notification is given for the purpose of uncovering such impediments as may stand in the way of the lawful ordination of the candidate.

Usually the announcement of the name and concomitant details

[93] Can. 1368. Cf. Cappello, *De Sacramentis*, II, Pars III, 512.
[94] Can. 994. § 2.
[95] *Commentarium*, III, *De Sacramentis*, 466.
[96] Can. 998, § 1.

is accomplished by word of mouth.[97] However, the ordinary enjoys the option of substituting a public posting of the announcement to the doors of the church for this customary method. If the substitution is made, the announcement remains posted for some days, one of which is a feast day. There is no need that this day be also a day of precept. As long as it is a day on which the faithful attend church in large numbers, the law is fulfilled. Moreover, there is no precise determination of the number of these days. Provided that the notice remains affixed for at least two days, the law is observed.

Unlike the oral announcement, there is no requirement that the posting be made in the parish church. At the time of the substitution there may be designated for this purpose any church within the jurisdiction of the pastor obliged to make the publication.

Roberts[98] shows that the phrase *"ad valvas"* is hardly to be understood in the most literal sense. Such an interpretation could easily lead to the defeat of the end of the law. If posted on the doors of the church, the announcement might be overlooked instead of being brought to the attention of the faithful. Consequently it seems that the posting of the announcement in a prominent place fulfills the law.

When the ordinary method is employed, the publication is made in church on a feast of precept, during the solemnities of the Mass, or on another day or at another hour when a large number of people gathers in the church.[99]

The days of precept include not only the feasts expressly listed in canon 1247, § 1, but also the Sundays of the year. If one or the other of these feasts is suppressed in a particular place, this day is excluded unless there is a large enough attendance to warrant the announcement. On the other hand, if the local ordinary in a particular instance for one set occasion establishes a day of precept,[100] the publication may be made then.

[97] Cf. I Synod of Fargo (1941), stat. 332—*Synodus Dioecesana Fargensis Prima, A.D. 1941 habita* (Milwaukee: Bruce, 1941), p. 65.

[98] *The Banns of Marriage*, p. 89.

[99] Can. 998, § 2: Publicatio fiat die festo de praecepto in ecclesia inter Missarum sollemnia aut alia die et hora quibus maior populi frequentia in ecclesia habeatur.

[100] Can. 1244, § 2.

Generally the notification is given within the solemnities of the Mass. Blat[101] interprets this to mean a sung or a parochial Mass. This does not seem to be an absolute necessity, since the important factor is the gathering of a large number of the faithful, and not the kind of ceremony they attend. That this is the mind of the legislator is clear from the latitude permitted by the last part of canon 998, § 3. If there is a notable assembly on another occasion, e.g., at Vespers, or at a mission, the announcement may be made then instead of at Mass. Certainly a change is preferable when a high Mass on Sunday or a day of precept is poorly attended.

What is said of the service at which the announcement is made is also true of the day itself. If a day not of precept is better suited to the end of the law, the publication may be undertaken then. This transfer is not dependent on the prudence of the ordinary, as are the other circumstance pertaining to the notification. The pastor may make the change from a day of precept and to a service other than that of the Holy Sacrifice.

No matter what the day or the hour selected, the ordination is announced in the church. This is a point on which canon 998 permits no choice. The reason for this is the obvious one that the faithful are presumed to be gathered there. The publication is then made for them in a manner befitting its importance and on an occasion permitting the necessary publicity.[102]

3. *Obligation of the Faithful*

The announcement of an impending ordination is the current method of seeking the opinion *(suffragium)* of the people concerning the candidates. When notification is given by the pastor, the faithful are obliged to reveal the impediments of which they know. They are disclosed to the ordinary or pastor before the actual ordination.[103] As it is quite likely that the faithful are unaware of this responsi-

[101] *Commentarium,* III, *De Sacramentis,* 467.

[102] Cf. Roberts, *The Banns of Marriage,* p. 84.

[103] Can. 999: Omnes fideles obligatione tenentur impedimenta ad sacros ordines, si qua norint, Ordinario vel parocho ante sacram ordinationem revelandi.

bility, there should be reference to it in the announcement. Otherwise the publication fails to achieve its end.[104] It also should be clear that they are to make known not only impediments in the strict sense but in the wider understanding as including anything arguing against the worthiness of the ordinand.[105]

4. *Dispensation*

The announcement of an ordination is of such a nature that it is dependent to a great extent on the prudence of the ordinary. Considering the circumstances, he may (a) for a just cause dispense from the publication; (b) command that it be made in other churches besides the parish church; (c) substitute a public affixture to the doors of the church.[106]

Although the pastor is obliged to make the announcement, dispensation is reserved to the ordinary. In this there is nothing unusual, since the pastor is acting for the ordinary, who estimates the worthiness of the candidate.

Canon 998, § 1, employs the word *"ordinarius"* without a determinant such as the words *"proprius"* or *"loci."* This occasions doubt concerning the identity of the ordinary who dispenses. The use of the unqualified term suggests that any ordinary obliged to give a judgment on the candidate may employ the publication as a means of supplementing his knowledge. However, an ordinary is usually only competent to dispense the pastors subject to himself. If the ordinand belongs to a parish in a diocese other than that of his proper ordinary, the ordinary where the parish is located may dispense from the announcement. May the proper ordinary do this? Does his

104 Instandum igitur ut banna suum finem non amittant, eo quod scrutinium de quo agitur efficaciter adiuvent; quapropter fideles instruendi et commonendi sunt, de onere gravissimo denuntiandi, si quid vocationi et ordinationi contrarium sciant, iuxta relatum can. 999. Et hoc valet tum pro irregularitatibus et impedimentis cuiusque generis sint, tum pro candidati vita et moribus . . .—Jorio, *Commentarius,* p. 103.

105 Cf. Conc. Trident., sess. XXIII, *de ref.,* c. 5; Cappello, *De Sacramentis,* II, Pars III, 513.

106 Can. 998, § 1.

power include not only his own territory but also all the parishes to which the aspirant is attached?

In canon 1029 there is express provision for a dispensation from the banns of marriage by the proper ordinary. For a legitimate cause he dispenses from the publication not only in his own but also in other dioceses. In the canons on ordination there is no mention of such an extension of power. The reason for this is that the rôle of an ordinary other than the proper one is far more important in the scrutiny prior to ordination than it is for matrimony.

For marriage the ordinary has discretionary powers relative to the investigation made in a place where the party resides for six months after attaining puberty.[107] No such freedom is granted in a similar situation for orders. Residence for a like period engenders a need for a testimonial from the ordinary of that place. No ordinary has the power to dispense from this obligation. Substitution of another form of proof in special situations is all that is permitted.[108]

To acquire the knowledge necessary for the granting of a testimonial the local ordinary may command that the announcement of the forthcoming ordination be made. Now, if the proper ordinary could dispense from this publication, a strange condition would exist. The local ordinary, obliged to send a testimonial to the proper ordinary, would be deprived of the power to formulate this letter by the very ordinary to whom it is to be sent.

There may be objection to this interpretation on the score that testimonials are sought before the reception of the first tonsure and the minor orders, while the publication takes place prior to the three major orders. This is the ordinary procedure, but it is by no means absolute. If a cleric spends a period of time in a place after ordination to the minor orders, the furnishing of a testimonial may be either mandatory or optional according to the prescriptions of canon 994, §§ 1, 3. Moreover, there is nothing to prevent the publication being made before the first tonsure and the minor orders. If an ordinary prefers to seek his information in this way, it seems that he should be allowed to do so without interference.

[107] Can. 1023, § 2.

[108] Can. 994, § 2. Cf. cans. 993, 4°; 994, §§ 1, 3.

If it is desirable that the announcement be made in a church that is not at present the parish church of the aspirant, the proper ordinary may only request this publication if the church is outside his own territory. He may indirectly force such an announcement by seeking a testimonial from the ordinary of that place. This latter ordinary is then obliged to testify concerning the worthiness of the candidate. To do this, it is more than likely that the pastor of the candidate's former residence has to be consulted.

When a dispensation from the announcement of a future imposition of hands is granted, it is in virtue of power explicitly given to the ordinary in canon 998, § 1. This power is applicable to a general law of the Church and is to be exercised in a particular case.[109]

What is the dispensatory power of custom? Cappello[110] contends that a custom of completely omitting the publications, without a particular dispensation granted by the ordinary for a just cause, is unreasonable. However, the status of being contrary to the Code does not immediately stamp a custom as unreasonable. If such a custom is centenary or immemorable at the time of the introduction of the present legislation, there is a possibility that its continuance may be tolerated. Such a continuance becomes permissible, however, only on the condition that the ordinary is of the opinion that the custom cannot prudently be displaced.[111] As Guilfoyle[112] demonstrates, this is not an arbitrary matter. An alteration in circumstances begets the obligation of having the law of the Code observed and the announcement of the forthcoming ordinations made.

When granted, a dispensation may extend to the publications for the three sacred orders, or it may be given for one or the other order. In all cases there has to be a just cause.[113] This cause is one which is of such a nature that it is reasonable and proportionate to the law

[109] Can. 81. Cf. Reilly, *The General Norms of Dispensation,* The Catholic University of America Canon Law Studies, n. 119 (Washington, D. C.: The Catholic University of America Press, 1939), p. 66.

[110] *De Sacramentis,* II, Pars III, 512.

[111] Can. 5.

[112] *Custom,* The Catholic University of America Canon Law Studies, n. 105 (Washington, D.C.: The Catholic University of America, 1937) p. 75.

[113] Cf. Reilly, *op. cit.,* pp. 107-13.

from which a dispensation is granted.[114] Continued residence at the seminary during the interstices and the outstanding character of the candidate seem to furnish a sufficient reason for such a dispensation.[115]

5. *Repetition*

The discretion of the ordinary also extends to the repetition of the announcement. Usually the passage of six months constitutes reason for another publication, but the ordinary may dispense from this if he has cause for doing so.[116] These months are computed according to the norms of canon 34, § 3, 1° and 3°, for the initial terminal point is expressed. They are also reckoned according to the calendar, beginning at midnight following the announcement and ending with the completion of the last day bearing the same date.

Although there is provision for a repetition within a definite period, there is no indication as to how long before the ordination the announcement is to be made. The same lacuna exists relative to the length of time the pastor should wait for the revelation of impediments after the announcement has been made. A reasonable interval of time, e.g., a month,[117] should be available before the ordination so that there may be enough time both to make the publication and to report the results to the ordinary. By allowing such a space of time it is also possible to investigate the impediments if any are reported.

To supply the other void, a norm may be drawn from the parallel case of marriage.[118] Thus a pastor waits for three days. If no impediments are revealed in that interval, the letter is sent to the ordinary.[119] Of course, if an impediment is reported after the testi-

[114] Can. 84, § 1.

[115] Cf. Blat, *Commentarium,* III, *De Sacramentis,* 466.

[116] Can. 998, § 3: Si sex intra menses candidatus promotus non fuerit, repetatur publicatio, nisi aliud Ordinario videatur.

[117] Cf. *Periodica,* V (1913), (14).

[118] Cf. cans. 20; 1030, § 1.

[119] Cf. Many, *De Sacra Ordinatione,* p. 305.

monial is forwarded, the pastor is obliged to transmit the new information to the ordinary.

B. *Supplementary Investigations*

Besides seeking information from the people by announcing future ordinations, the ordinary undertakes another inquiry into the character and life of the candidate. There is entrusted to the pastor who makes the publication and also to another, if it is expedient, the task of diligently questioning trustworthy men concerning the status of the ordinand.[120]

This prescription further emphasizes the rôle of the pastor. His position as an adviser of the ordinary is of prime importance in this regard. As the rector of the seminary is the best judge of the aspirant when the latter is under his observation, so the office of the pastor enables him to appraise the candidate as a resident within parochial boundaries. The present situation whereby not all seminaries have summer villas adds importance to this position of the pastor. When it is necessary that the students return to their homes during the summer months, a particular vigilance is exercised over them by the pastor.[121]

According to Blat,[122] the pastor who makes the announcement is always commissioned for the investigation commanded by canon 1000, § 1. This is not absolutely correct. The bishop seeks this in-

[120] Can. 1000, § 1: Parocho qui publicationem peragit, et etiam alii, si id expedire videatur, Ordinarius committat ut de ordinandorum moribus et vita a fide dignis diligenter exquirat, et litteras testimoniales, ipsam investigationem et publicationem referentes, ad Curiam transmittat.

[121] Cf. III Plenary Council of Baltimore (1884), tit. V, *De clericorum educatione*, c. *De seminariis majoribus*, n. 177—*Acta et Decreta Concilii Plenarii Baltimorensis Tertii, A.D. MDCCCLXXXIV* (Baltimorae, 1886), p. 90; I Synod of Fargo (1941), stat. 330—*Synodus Dioecesana Fargensis Prima*, p. 64; *Letter of the Apostolic Delegate to the Bishops of the United States*, 5 May, 1935; Barrett, *A Comparative Study of the Councils of Baltimore and the Code of Canon Law*, The Catholic University of America Canon Law Studies, n. 83 (Washington, D. C.: The Catholic University of America, 1932), p. 175.

[122] *Commentarium*, III, *De Sacramentis*, 467.

formation rather from another pastor or priest in that territory under certain conditions, e.g., if the pastor and candidate are related.[123] This is especially true if sacred orders are to be received with a dispensation from the publications or before they are complete.[124]

On first sight the wording of canon 1000, § 1, conveys the impression that this part of the examination of the ordinand is not undertaken until he is to receive sacred orders. The designation of the pastor making the publication as the usual agent for the inquiry engenders this notion. However, it seems more correct to say that this designation, with reference to the announcement, is employed as a device to indicate who is delegated and not necessarily the time of delegation. Certainly it is a simpler mode of expression than one determining delegation on the basis of the origin or domiciles of the candidate. It is the pastor determined in this way who investigates not only for the major but also for the minor orders. The Instruction *Quam ingens*[125] employs this latter interpretation in proposing norms, based on this canon, to be followed by the bishop and the pastor preparatory to the conferring of the first tonsure and the minor orders.

In general the ordinary commissions the pastor to make a thorough inquiry into the virtues and the signs of a vocation in the candidate as well as concerning his past and present manner of life. Special attention is given to the conduct of the aspirant during the period of vacation, and there is also the consideration of the reputation and condition of his family and its attitude toward the ordination.[126] It suffices if this phase of the examination is undertaken only once. When the candidate is to receive sacred orders, there is no need again to inquire into his origin, the condition and character of his parents, and the nature of his former life unless the evidence at hand is now suspect.[127]

123 Cf. Gasparri, *De Sacra Ordinatione*, nn. 679, 694, 699; Jorio, *Commentarius*, pp. 121-2.

124 *Quam ingens*, § 2, n. 7—*AAS*, XXIII (1931), 123.

125 § 2, n. 6—*AAS*, XXIII (1931), 123.

126 *Loc. cit.* Cf. Larraona, "Animadversiones," *Apollinaris*, IV (1931), 209; Jorio, *Commentarius*, pp. 120-1.

127 *Quam ingens*, § 3, n. 1—*AAS*, XXIII (1931), 125.

The particular considerations regarding the aspirant, on which the testimonal of the pastor is founded, are indicated in an appendix to the Instruction *Quam ingens*[128] and are substantially as follows: the possibility of inheriting parental abnormalities, particularly in matters of sex; his devotion, especially in hearing Mass, in visiting the Blessed Sacrament and in reciting the Rosary; his reception of the sacraments of penance and the Eucharist; his attitude toward the exercise and in the performance of sacred functions; his application in teaching Christian doctrine (a work to which the ordinand is assigned before receiving sacred orders); his zeal for the worship of God and the care of souls; his interest in study; the nature of the material he reads; the use of clerical dress; his associations, both of persons and places; his attitude toward boys, girls and adult persons of the other sex; his inclination toward the comforts of life, particularly alcoholic beverages; the respect he shows to superiors; the public opinion of his vocation; his freedom from compulsion in aspiring to the priesthood.

Besides these points of the Instruction *Quam ingens,* the pastor in the United States is also to be mindful of the recommendations of the Sacred Congregation for Seminaries and Universities, as expressed in the letter of the Apostolic Delegate to the bishops of this country on May 5, 1935. In addition to some of the points already noted, this communication stresses the general need for care during the summer months. In this respect the pastor exercises special vigilance. He must be well-informed and submit a confidential report on the candidate. This statement should "cover the general conduct of the seminarians during the vacation period and in particular their faithfulness to spiritual duties. The parish-priests shall also add any remarks which may be proper in a particular case."[129] Under this latter heading is included reference to the type of work done by the seminarians during the summer, especially if the position is such as is "not in keeping with the dignity or the spirit of their holy vocation,"[130]e.g., driving a taxi-cab, holding a position in a hotel, etc.[131]

[128] *Ibid.,* p. 128.
[129] *Letter of the Apostolic Delegate,* May 5, 1935, § 7.
[130] *Ibid.,* Introduction.
[131] *Ibid.,* § 1.

Besides the pastors, others may be interrogated for special information. These persons, ecclesiastical and secular, should be trustworthy and not prejudiced in favor of or against the candidate.[132] This part of the examination is optional and is undertaken by the ordinary as circumstances dictate. It is particularly recommended when there is some doubt of the character and canonical suitableness of the aspirant.[133] These persons are usually questioned concerning the behavior of the candidate, his vocation, the attitude of his family, his associates, and his reputation.[134]

In addition to the above mentioned inquiry the ordinary is also obliged to undertake another investigation if this is thought necessary or opportune.[135] This is more confidential in nature and is made by the ordinary himself or a person chosen by the ordinary without consideration of his official capacity.

On the completion of these investigations, as well as the publication, the information collected is forwarded to the curia. This report contains the substance of the findings and an indication of their value.[136] Even if the results are purely negative, the pastor and the other investigators send a letter attesting to this fact. In this way the responsible ordinary is assured both that the prescriptions of the law are fulfilled and that he is sufficiently informed to judge the candidate.[137] These data are kept on file in the curia together with the other documents pertaining to ordination.[138]

[132] Cf. Blat, *Commentarium*, III, *De Sacramentis*, 468.

[133] *Quam ingens*, § 2, n. 8—*AAS*, XXIII (1931), 124.

[134] *Ibid.*, p. 129.

[135] Can. 1000, § 2: Idem Ordinarius alias percontationes etiam privatas, si id necessarium aut opportunum iudicaverit, facere ne omittat.

[136] Blat, *Commentarium*, III, *De Sacramentis*, 468.

[137] Cf. Cappello, *De Sacramentis*, II, Pars III, 514.

[138] Can. 1010, § 1; *Quam ingens*, § 1, n. 5—*AAS*, XXIII (1931), 122.

CHAPTER V

EXAMINATION OF RELIGIOUS CANDIDATES

Article I. *Non-Exempt Religious*

A. *Subjection to the Law of Seculars*

Canon 993 applies to the religious who are governed for ordination by the law of seculars. Those so obligated are determined by the status of their institute as exempt or non-exempt.[1] Exempt religious follow special norms for the reception of orders,[2] while the non-exempt are regulated by the law established for seculars.[3] Congregations in the latter category are specified as (1) non-exempt institutes in which perpetual profession is made; (2) non-exempt congregations in which there is temporary profession renewable on its expiration; (3) societies of men living in common without vows.[4] The last mentioned, although they are not religious in the stricter understanding of the term, are in many respects governed as religious[5] and in virtue of canon 251, § 1, are included within the competence of the Sacred Congregation for Religious.[6] As long as the

[1] Cf. cans. 615; 488, 2°, 7°; Cappello, *De Sacramentis,* II, Pars III, 266; *Periodica,* IX (1921), (16)-(18); Schaaf, "Episcopus Proprius Ordinationis Religiosorum," *The American Ecclesiastical Review* (formerly *The Ecclesiastical Review,* Philadelphia, 1889-1943; Baltimore, 1944-), XC (1934), 498.

[2] Cf. cans. 964; 995.

[3] Cf. cans. 964; 993.

[4] Cf. cans. 488, 1°; 678; Schaaf, *art. cit.,* pp. 498-509; Moeder, *The Proper Bishop for Ordination and Dimissorial Letters,* p. 107; McBride, *Incardination and Excardination of Seculars,* p. 343.

[5] Cans. 673-681.

[6] Cf. *Quantum Religiones,* n. 15—*AAS,* XXIV (1932), 80; Coetus S.R.E. Cardinalium a Summo Pontifice peculiariter designatus, 24 mart. 1919—*AAS,* XI (1919), 251; Maroto, "Annotationes," *Commentarium pro Religiosis* (later [1935]*Commentarium pro Religiosis et Missionariis,* Romae, 1920-), II (1921), 101; XIII (1932), 176.

institutes in these classes do not possess an indult or privilege of exemption or a grant conferring the power to issue a dimissorial, they are under the law of seculars for the reception of orders.[7]

In these non-exempt societies none of the superiors has the power of an ordinary. They must look beyond the organization for this authority. In fact, for ordination the various members may have different proper ordinaries who are also distinct from the local ordinary to whom the religious house itself is subject.

The proper bishop for the ordination of the perpetually professed religious is the ordinary of the diocese in which the house of his attachment is situated. The domicile this candidate has in the world is lost by perpetual profession.[8] and he is now considered as being domiciled in the place of the house to which he is assigned. It is the ordinary of this territory who lawfully ordains the religious or grants him a dimissorial.[9]

Religious temporarily professed are likewise regulated by the law of seculars. The ordinand in this category differs from one perpetually professed in that he still is linked to the original or acquired domicile possessed prior to his entry in religion.[10] It is the ordinary of this domicile who is the proper bishop for ordination or for the concession of a dimissorial.

Finally, there are the institutes of men without vows. Unless exempted, these members are ordained after the manner of seculars.[11] They never lose the proper bishop of the domicile possessed prior to affiliation with the institute.[12] In this they differ from the perpetually

[7] Cf. Vermeersch-Creusen, *Epitome,* II, 182; Fanfani, *De Iure Religiosorum ad Normam Cordicis Iuris Canonici* (ed. 2, Taurini-Romae: Marietti, 1925), p. 319; Goyeneche, "Consultationes," *CpR,* VIII (1927), 378; Moeder, *op. cit.,* p. 109; McBride, *loc. cit.*

[8] Can. 585.

[9] Cf. cans. 964, 4°; 956; Schaaf, "Episcopus Proprius Ordinationis Religiosorum," *AER,* XC (1934), 499; Moeder, *op. cit.,* p. 108; McBride, *op. cit.,* p. 344.

[10] Cf. can. 585; McBride, *loc. cit.:* Schaaf, *art. cit.,* pp. 501, 504.

[11] Can. 678. Cf. Schäfer, *De Religiosis ad Normam Codicis Iuris Canonici* (Münster: Aschendorff, 1927), p. 619.

[12] Vermeersch-Creusen, *Epitome,* I, 615; McBride, *loc. cit.;* Schaaf, *art. cit.,* p. 505.

professed religious, although, for the most part, both are governed for ordination by the same norms. The proper bishop for these men who are living in common without vows is the ordinary of the place of birth, if they still have a domicile there, or of the place of domicile at the time of their entry in the society.[13]

The determination of the proper bishop for the ordination of the non-exempt is particularly important because he is the ordinary who ultimately judges whether or not the candidate has the required canonical qualities and is free of irregularities and other impediments.[14] Because of the obligation to make this judgment it seems that there should be strict adherence to the provisions of canon 993. The attestations and testimonials specified there are to be sent to this ordinary for his guidance. Confirmatory of this procedure is the norm enunciated by canon 960, § 1. This canon demands that all the documents of canons 993-1000 be at hand before a dimissorial is issued. Since the local ordinary concedes the letter, when one is granted for these religious, should he not have these testimonies?

This is not to be interpreted as a restriction of the rights of the authorities of the institute. As the ordinary has his sphere for judgment, so also do the religious superiors. They form, approve, and select their subjects for ordination even as a bishop does.[15] However, there is this difference in the rôles of the two authorities: The ordinary is the absolute judge of the worthiness of his subjects, whereas the decisions of the superior of an institute which is not exempt are conditioned by the findings of the proper ordinary.

The position of the ordinary in the investigation is emphasized in the case of religious who do not have perpetual vows. These ordinands are obliged by canon 998, so that their names should be announced in the parish church before their reception of sacred orders. The result of this inquiry is then forwarded to the curia and added to the other data on which the ordinary makes his judgment. It is true that the perpetually professed, even those ruled by the law of seculars, are excused from the ruling of canon 998, but this is

[13] Can. 956.

[14] Cf. can. 968, § 1.

[15] *Quantum Religiones,* n. 12—*AAS,* XXIV (1932), 78.

because they no longer have a proper diocese or parish.[16] However, it seems that even in the case of these religious the ordinary is free to undertake the investigations of canon 1000, § 2.

B. *Testimonials Required*

1. *Local Ordinaries*

In adhering to the legislation applicable to seculars, non-exempt religious must produce testimonials from the ordinaries in whose territory they resided long enough to contract a canonical impediment, i.e., three or six months, as depending on circumstances.[17] For the most part these local ordinaries are the same as those who were approached before the candidate's admission to the religious institute. Consequently there is question as to whether or not the testimonials granted to the postulant are acceptable at the time of ordination. In some respects these letters are very much alike. Their content is concerned with the character and life of the candidate, particularly his freedom from irregularities and canonical impediments, and the testimony is given only after a diligent inquiry that extends even to a private investigation.[18]

Although this parallel does exist, there are important aspects under which differences are noted. The testimonials given to the postulant are those which are issued to all male candidates for entry in religion, while the letters granted to an ordinand are issued precisely for the reception of orders.[19] To maintain that the letters differ in this respect is to continue recognition for a distinction emphasized prior to the Code.[20]

That the demands in the case of ordination are more exacting is clear from a consideration of the temporal basis for the testimonials. The postulant in religion, even though he was a soldier, has only to obtain letters from the ordinaries of his place of origin and of any

[16] Can. 585.

[17] Cans. 993, 4°; 994, § 1.

[18] Cf. cans. 545, § 4; 994, § 2; 1000.

[19] Cf. Goyeneche, "Consultationes," *CpR*, III (1922), 263; Vermeersch-Creusen, *Epitome*, II, 182.

[20] Cf. S.C.C., *Pientina, seu Ilcinen.*, 8 aug. 1733—*Thesaurus*, VI, 125.

other place where his residence after attaining the fourteenth year was prolonged for a twelvemonth.[21] The stricter law for ordination demands a testimonial from any ordinary in whose territory the candidate remained long enough, i.e., three or six months,[22] to make possible the contracting of a canonical impediment.[23] It is obvious that instances occur in which no testimonial is needed for entry in religion, but is required for ordination, e.g., when a candidate remains in a place between six and twelve months.[24]

Blat[25] is of the opinion that the testimonials granted prior to entry in religion are so efficacious that no new letters are required before ordination. He errs in identifying the testimonials of canons 544, § 2, and 545, § 4, with those of canon 993, 4°. Blat makes the statement without attempting to reconcile the differences apparent in the two types of testimonial letters.

Although the earlier testimonials are unacceptable in relation to the reception of orders, there are situations in which the testimonials granted for entry in religion may be utilized for the later ordination. This is the case when the local ordinary testifies expressly that the candidate for the institute is free of any irregularity or impediment that might interfere with his reception of orders. In such instances the context of the letter is scrutinized and the element of time is considered. If both conform to the law for ordinations the letter is a sufficient attestation.

The procedure outlined in the preceding paragraph is admissible when the candidate has remained in the same diocese for the entire period intervening between his attainment of puberty and his subsequent association with the religious institute. However, if he has moved about from place to place, there has to be a check not only as bearing on the context of the letters but also as certifying that the temporal requirements of canon 994, § 1, have been satisfied.

21 Can. 544, § 2.

22 Can. 994, § 1.

23 Can. 993, 4°.

24 Cf. Larraona, "Commentarium Codicis," *CpRM*, XIX (1938), 158.

25 *Commentarium*, III, *De Sacramentis*, 458.

2. *Major Superiors*

Besides the usual testimonials required of seculars, the religious ordinand must also have a letter from his major superior.[26] Unless the religious is presented for ordination in this way, there is no need for further consideration of his application.

The major superiors with this power of presentation are enumerated in canon 488, 8°. It is an indiscriminate listing that includes the superiors for those enjoying exemption as well as for those who are governed relative to ordination by the law of seculars.[27] Among them, the supreme moderator of the institute, a provincial superior, their vicars, and those having power in the manner of a provincial are the authorities ordinarily found in non-exempt societies. They may issue the necessary testimonial, whereas the minor superiors lack authority and may proceed to act only when delegated.[28]

These major superiors are not ordinaries in the proper understanding of the term.[29] They lack jurisdiction, and this must be supplied by a local ordinary. If ever the designation of ordinary is applied to them, it is done so only indirectly and because of a special power given in a certain matter.[30]

The additional question now arises as to whether or not the major superior of a lay institute is to be included among the major superiors referred to by canon 993, 5°. It seems that they are, for the canon itself makes no distinction. Nor does the nature of the matter necessarily exclude them. The society itself may be under

[26] Canon 993, 5°.

[27] Cf. Schäfer, *De Religiosis,* pp. 47-8; Berutti, *Institutiones Iuris Canonici* (6 vols., Vol. III, Taurini-Romae: Marietti, 1936), III, *De Religiosis,* 16; Larraona, "Commentarium Codicis," *CpR,* IV (1923), 39-46.

[28] Cf. Berutti, *loc. cit.;* Larraona, *art. cit.,* p. 39; Clancy, *The Local Religious Superior,* The Catholic University of America Canon Law Studies, n. 175 (Washington, D. C.: The Catholic University of America Press, 1943), pp. 163-4.

[29] Can. 198, § 1.

[30] Cf. S.C. Consist., decr. *Redeuntibus,* 25 oct. 1918—*AAS,* X (1918), 481-6; 20 ian. 1919—*AAS,* XI (1919), 43; "Annotationes," *Periodica,* IX (1921), 132; X (1922), 46; Larraona, "Quaestio Canonica," *CpR.* IV (1923), 113-9.

the jurisdiction of the local ordinary, but the same situation exists for many of the clerical institutes. In neither case is this ordinary considered to be a major superior[31] but in both instances the relative powers of the superiors within the congregation are the same. Certainly there is nobody in a better position than the religious superior to judge the candidate.[32]

Although lacking the capacity to testify as ordinaries,[33] the major religious superior does attest to certain facts and qualities pertinent to the ordinand. These are not expressly indicated in canon 993, 5°, but may be drawn from other canons and from the very nature of his position as a major superior in presenting one of his subjects for ordination.

In granting a testimonial the major superior is necessarily limited to his own subjects. The primary requisite, therefore, is an indication in the letter that the candidate is a member of the institute in which the grantor of the testimonial is a superior.[34] Then there is an expression of the status of the ordinand within the society. He may not be a novice,[35] and to receive major orders he must be perpetually professed.[36] The superiors may present non-exempt religious of temporary profession for the first tonsure and the minor orders, but not for the major orders.[37] If there is question of a congregation in which only temporary vows are taken, the first tonsure and the minor orders may be received during the first triennial period. When the vows are renewed the advance to the major orders may be made. In the case of societies of men without vows, the members are eligible for sacred orders only on completion of three years of affiliation with the institute.[38]

Besides the facts of membership in the community and the

[31] Cf. can. 488, 8°.

[32] Cf. Vermeersch-Creusen, *Epitome,* II, 166; Fanfani, *De Iure Religiosorum,* p. 319.

[33] Cf. *L'Ami du Clergé* (Paris, 1878-), XLVI (1929), 410.

[34] Cf. can. 995, § 1; *Quantum Religiones,* n. 12—*AAS,* XXIV (1932), 78.

[35] Can. 567, § 2.

[36] Cf. can. 964, 4°.

[37] Can. 964, 4°. Cf. *Quantum Religiones,* n. 15—*AAS,* XXIV (1932), 80.

[38] *Quantum Religiones, loc. cit.*

status of the ordinand relative to profession or permanent association with the society, the superior is fully competent to testify concerning the character of the aspirant. By reason of his position he has a wealth of material on which to draw for forming this judgment. Basically this consists of the data compiled at the time when the member was received into the community. From the outset he is considered with a view to the future reception of orders. Because of this there is a diligent preparatory investigation of his disposition, ability and character,[39] and a careful consideration of the reasons motivating his entry in religion.[40] In the very beginning there must be signs of a divine vocation.[41]

The family of the postulant is also investigated to ascertain whether or not there is any likelihood of his inheriting parental vices.

Before admission to simple vows the novice must declare in writing his calling to the religious and clerical state and his resolve forever to serve as a cleric in the religious life.[42]

When orders are to be conferred, superiors[43] are to present nobody before making a careful examination of the character, piety, modesty, chastity, inclination to the clerical life, and progress both in study and in religious discipline on the part of the candidate.[44] For this information the *magister spiritus* and others conversant with the life and character of the student are consulted.[45] A record of this inquiry is preserved in the archives. Finally, the superior him-

[39] Cans. 544; 545.

[40] *Quantum Religiones,* n. 4—*AAS,* XXIV (1932), 75.

[41] Cf. cans. 973, § 1; 1363, § 1; *Quantum Religiones,* n. 6—*AAS,* XXIV (1932), 76; Vermeersch, "Annotationes," *Periodica,* XXI (1932), 188.

[42] *Quantum Religiones,* n. 14—*AAS,* XXIV (1932), 79. Cf. Vermeersch, *art. cit.,* 191.

[43] Note: The Instruction *Quantum Religiones* employs this general designation without distinguishing major and minor superiors. From canon 993, 5°, it is clear that the major superior is to grant the testimonial, but others may be delegated to gather the required data. Cf. can. 199, § 1; Goyeneche, "Consultationes," *CpRM,* XIX (1938), 17.

[44] Cf. can. 973, § 1; *Quantum Religiones,* n. 14—*AAS,* XXIV (1932), 79.

[45] Cf. can. 588; Vermeersch, "Annotationes," *Periodica,* XXI (1932), 192; *Quantum Religiones, loc. cit.*

self or through another questions the aspirant concerning his freedom in seeking ordination.[46]

Prior to the reception of the subdiaconate there is another investigation similar to that described above. The results of the former inquiry are compared with the new findings, so that the progress or retrogression of the candidate may be noted. If he is then considered worthy, the religious is presented for ordination according to the norms of canon law and the constitutions of the institute.[47] In this regard the superiors have an obligation comparable to that of the bishop, so that they must be morally certain of the suitableness of the ordinand.[48]

The final requisite before advancement to the subdiaconate is the signing by the candidate of the declaration prescribed by the Sacred Congregation for Religious.[49] In presenting the candidate the superior is to testify to this as well as to the signing of the petition before the profession.[50]

For the diaconate and priesthood the information required is not so comprehensive, but the superior must be vigilant during the interstices lest anything arise to cause doubt concerning the vocation of the candidate. Should doubt arise, or should it become clear that the religious is not called to the clerical state, the matter is referred to the Sacred Congregation for Religious.[51]

This concern of the religious superiors for the moral training of their subjects is but one aspect of their obligation. They also must provide for the intellectual life of the candidates so as to be able to testify to the completion of the studies required for the reception of orders. This interest antedates the immediate preparation for ordination. Before admitting postulants to religion the funda-

[46] *Quantum Religiones, loc. cit.*

[47] *Ibid.*, n. 16—*AAS*, XXIV (1932), 80.

[48] Cf. can. 973, § 3; *Quantum Religiones*, n. 13—*AAS*, XXIV (1932), 79; Maroto, "Annotationes," *CpR*, XIII (1932), 178.

[49] *Quantum Religiones*, n. 17—*AAS*, XXIV (1932), 80.

[50] *Ibid.*, n. 19—*AAS*, XXIV (1932), 81.

[51] Can. 251, § 1; *Quantum Religiones*, n. 20—*AAS*, XXIV (1932), 81.

mental requirements relative to studies must be satisfied.[52]

When ordination is imminent non-exempt religious must produce an attestation as to the studies undertaken for each order.[53] This entails no particular difficulty when the clerical institute has a house of studies approved by its general chapter or superiors.[54] In this *studium* the religious are instructed in philosophy and theology preparatory to the reception of orders.[55] The house of studies is the equivalent of the secular seminary with the added note that the students are prepared not only for the clerical state but also for the religious mode of life. As far as studies are concerned, the two dovetail and the exactions of canon 976 must be satisfied by the students of both the seminary and the *studium*.

If the province has no house of studies proper to itself, the religious is sent to one in another province, to a secular seminary, or to the *studium* of another institute.[56] In all these instances the rector of the school is competent to testify to the studies completed for each order. His report is forwarded to the major superior who grants the testimonial including these data.[57]

Whether or not the more rigid pre-Code legislation regarding the studies of religious[58] is still in force is disputed. In a recent work Bolduc[59] thoroughly examines the question and his concurrence with Oesterle[60] and Larraona[61] seems to be the more probable solu-

[52] Cf. can. 589, § 1; Pius XI, ep. ap. *Unigenitus,* 19 mart. 1924—*AAS,* XVI (1924), 140; *Quantum Religiones,* n. 5—*AAS,* XXIV (1932), 75; Vermeersch, "Annotationes," *Periodica,* XXI (1932), 190.

[53] Can. 993, 2°.

[54] Can. 587, § 1.

[55] Can. 589, § 1.

[56] Can. 587, § 3.

[57] *Quantum Religiones,* n. 12: Hisce testimonialibus litteris Superior religiosus non solum alumos esse de familia testatur, sed etiam de studiis peractis, deque aliis in iure requisitis fidem facit.—*AAS,* XXIV (1932), 78.

[58] S.C. de Rel., declar. 7 sept. 1909—*Fontes,* n. 4397; 31 maii 1910—*Fontes,* n. 4402.

[59] *Les Études dans les Religions Cléricales,* pp. 88-97.

[60] "De ratione studiorum in religionibus clericalibus," *CpR,* VI (1925), 308-9.

[61] "Consultationes," *CpR,* V (1924), 103-4.

tion. This opinion maintains that the declarations of 1909 and 1910 feature prescriptions omitted from the Code in the general reorganization of this matter.[62] Consequently, when the present legislation establishes a general norm regarding the studies necessary for ordination,[63] this is applicable not only to seculars but also to religious.

If the institute enjoys the privilege of presenting its subjects for ordination at the end of the third year of theology,[64] then proof of this is furnished either by a copy of the document or through the constitutions of the society. The bishop may then proceed to ordain without observance of the regulation of canon 976, § 2. Such a privilege usually permits the reception of the subdiaconate on the conclusion of the first year of theology, and of the diaconate at the end of the second.

C. *Attestations Required*

As for the first tonsure, so also for admission to a religious society an attestation to baptism is required.[65] This may be supplied either by a certificate or by the other methods already described.[66] However, if the oath of the candidate is accepted at the time of his entry in religion, greater proof is to be furnished before his presentation for the first tonsure.

When the proper bishop for ordination is someone other than the ordinary in whose territory the sacrament of baptism was administered to the candidate, there is question as to whether or not it is necessary that the certificate be forwarded to the proper ordinary. Is the law satisfied if the major superior merely states that the ordinand is baptized, or that he has all the canonical requirements?

It is the opinion of the writer that in such a case either the certificate or a transcript is to be sent to the ordinary. This is due to the absence of distinction in canon 993, 1° even though it is ap-

[62] Cf. Vermeersch, "Annotationes," *Periodica,* XXI (1932), 190.

[63] Cans. 976; 993, 2°.

[64] Cf. S.C. de Rel., declar. 27 oct. 1923—*AAS,* XV (1923), 156.

[65] Cans. 993, 1°; 544, § 1.

[66] Cf. *supra,* Chap. III, art. II, A.

plicable both to seculars and non-exempt religious. Moreover, canon 960, § 1, is absolute in its demands that the necessary testimonies be at hand before a dimissorial is issued. The statement of the religious superior fails to fulfill this requisite inasmuch as his declaration is not an authentic attestation to the baptism of the candidate.

What is said of baptism is also applicable to confirmation. Proof of the fact may be supplied in various ways but, no matter what the procedure, an authentic statement is to be forwarded to the proper ordinary if the administration of the sacrament is not recorded in his diocesan or parochial archives.[67]

If the religious is elevated to orders by his proper bishop for ordination there is no need to furnish proof when he again becomes an ordinand. The record is available to the bishop in his own archives. This is also true when the candidate is ordained with a dimissorial letter. In this case the document which he receives after ordination is shown to the proper ordinary in order that the fact may be registered in the archives.[68] For a future promotion or dimissorial the proper bishop has only to advert to this record for satisfactory proof of the reception of the order immediately preceding the one now desired.

Under certain conditions there may be a variation in this procedure. It may have happened that the religious was the recipient of the first tonsure and of the minor orders while he was still temporarily professed. At perpetual profession he loses the former diocesan domicile, and the proper bishop for future ordinations is then the ordinary of the place where the religious house is situated. When the candidate is first presented to this latter bishop for ordination, proof of the last ordination must be advanced, for this ordinary is uninformed concerning the status of the candidate. This situation supposes, of course, that the aspirant is in a house located in a territory other than that of his former domicile.

These testimonials and attestations are expressly demanded by the law of ordination for seculars. Are any others needed by religious who are governed by this legislation? It seems not, at least in

[67] Cf. can. 470, §§ 1, 3.
[68] Can. 1010, § 2.

so far as the examination of the qualities of the candidate is concerned. It is true that the major superior must issue an attestation relative to the retreat to be made before ordination.[69] However, this is not expressly considered here, since it is extraneous to a study of the qualities of the ordinand.

Article II. *Exempt Religious*

A. *Exemption from the Law of Seculars*

As distinct from the non-exempt, the subjects of this article are those who are not obligated as to ordination to the law of seculars. Included here are not only the institutes enjoying exemption through the common law[70] or a papal privilege, but also those who are in possession of an indult empowering their superiors to grant dimissorial letters to their subjects.[71] In fact, the subjects may not be ordained without these dimissorials.[72]

It is common to all the exempt that they are in varying degrees withdrawn from the jurisdiction of the local ordinary and are regulated by special norms emanating from the Holy See.[73] This basis for distinction groups the exempt in the following categories: (1) regulars, i.e., those who make profession of vows in an order, or those who belong to an institute in which at least some members take solemn vows;[74] (2) religious of a congregation that is exempt through papal privilege;[75] (3) members of a society, not exempt through the common law or a papal privilege, but enjoying partial

69 Can. 1001, § 4.

70 Cf. O'Brien, *The Exemption of Religious in Church Law* (Milwaukee: Bruce, 1943), p. 9.

71 Hoc igitur signo, religiosi qui proprio iure reguntur ab iis qui saecularium iure obnoxii sunt, distinguuntur, quod priores a propriis Superioribus dimissorias litteras accipiunt.—Vermeersch-Creusen, *Epitome,* II, 182.

72 Can. 964, 2°. Cf. Blat, *Commentarium,* III, *De Sacramentis,* 376.

73 Cf. Maroto, *Institutiones Iuris Canonici ad Normam Novi Codicis* (2 vols., tom. I, Matriti, 1919), I, n. 728; O'Brien, *op. cit.,* pp. 3, 24.

74 Cans. 488, 2°, 7°; 615. Cf. Schäfer, *De Religiosis,* p. 43; Berutti, *De Religiosis,* p. 14; McBride, *Incardination and Excardination of Seculars,* p. 343.

75 Cans. 488, 2°, 7°; 618, § 1.

exemption in that it possesses an indult authorizing a superior to grant a dimissorial.[76]

B. *Dimissorial Letter Required*

1. *Grantor of the Letter*

That members of the above religions be ordained lawfully, it is necessary that a prelate having the necessary power be designated for this purpose by a superior of the society. Who is the superior competent to do this? Canon 995, § 1,[77] employs the general term "*Superior*" without specifying his precise authority in the institute. Does this mean that any superior in an institute, exempt at least for the reception of orders, is able to grant the dimissorial?

Unlike canon 995, § 1, canon 964, 2°, is explicit. It expressly states that exempt religious are not lawfully ordained by a bishop unless a dimissorial letter is conceded by their major superior.[78] Certainly included in this designation are the supreme moderators and provincials.[79] The former may grant a dimissorial for all the members of the organization, while the latter, as other major superiors ruling over a part of the society, are restricted to their own subjects.[80]

Is the word "*Superior*" of canon 995, § 1, to be interpreted strictly in the light of canon 964, 2°? In other words, is a major superior the only one who issues a dimissorial, or are there instances when the local superior may do so?

Prior to the Code there were cases in which the local superior

[76] Wernz-Vidal, *Ius Canonicum,* tom. IV, *De Rebus,* I, 248; Fanfani, *De Iure Religiosorum,* p. 319; McBride, *loc. cit.;* Moeder, *The Proper Bishop for Ordination and Dimissorial Letters,* p. 102; Goyeneche, "Consultationes," *CpR,* VIII (1927), 376-8; Voltas, "De domicilio quoad ordinationem religiosorum," *CpR,* II (1921), 301.

[77] Etiam Superior religiosus suis litteris dimissoriis non solum testari debet promovendum professionem religiosam emisisse et esse de familia domus religiosae sibi subditae, sed etiam de studiis peractis, deque aliis iure requisitis.

[78] Can. 964, 2°: Religiosi exempti a nullo Episcopo ordinari licite possunt sine litteris dimissoriis proprii Superioris maioris.

[79] Can. 488, 8°.

[80] Cappello, *De Sacramentis,* II, Pars III, 298; Goyeneche, *art. cit.,* p. 377.

of exempt religious legitimately granted this letter.[81] May he continue this practice under the current legislation? Fanfani[82] unreservedly answers in the negative, but Cappello,[83] on the other hand, distinguishes the source of this power in the superior. If it originates in a particular indult or an apostolic privilege, it is still operative according to the norms of canon 4; if it is based on the constitutions of the institute, it is abrogated. To the writer it appears that the opinion of Cappello is correct. Thus, the local superior remains competent to concede a dimissorial if his authority to do so is rooted in a privilege or indult existing at the time of the promulgation of the Code. The present law does not expressly revoke such an indult or privilege. If the constitutions of the society furnish the complete basis for this power, the local superior may no longer issue the letter. His ability to do so is precluded by reason of canon 6, 1°, for in this latter case it is founded on a particular law opposed to the prescripts of the Code.

An additional question concerns the ability of the superiors of exempt lay institutes. Do the terms *"superior"* and *"major superior"* apply to them in the present case? If a member of the Knights Hospitallers of St. John is to be ordained, may his superior issue the necessary dimissorial? It is the common opinion of authors, e.g., Fanfani,[84] Vermeersch-Creusen,[85] Cappello[86] and Saucedo,[87] that the lay superior is competent. The fundamental reason alleged is that canon 964, 2°, does not distinguish between major superiors of clerical and lay institutes.

81 Cf. Gasparri, *De Sacra Ordinatione*, nn. 743-4; 918-9; Clancy, *The Local Religious Superior*, p. 163.

82 *De Iure Religiosorum*, p. 319.

83 *Loc. cit.*

84 *Loc. cit.*

85 *Epitome*, II, 162.

86 *Loc. cit.*

87 "Exercitium Jurisdictionis et Superiores Laici ex Ordine Hospitalario S. Joannis de Deo," *CpR*, XIII (1932), 51-61, 106-14, 224-31, 191-302. This is a comprehensive treatment concerning the possibility and exercise of jurisdiction in this particular lay institute.

2. *Content of the Letter*

Prior to the Code there was a general declaration of the necessity of the superior's attesting to the fitness of the candidate.[88] Authors such as Gasparri[89] and Many[90] interpreted this to mean that the grantor of a dimissorial have testimony to the parentage, age, baptism, confirmation, studies, religious profession, residence, examination on knowledge, and the last ordination of the aspirant. In the present law there is a statement somewhat more precise than that of the old legislation, but not as compendious as the interpretations of the commentators cited. According to the Code, the religious superior testifies in his letter, not only to the religious profession of the candidate and his membership in a religious house subject to the superior, but also concerning his studies and the other legal requisites.[91]

In considering the content of the dimissorial, Sipos,[92] Papi[93] and Stadtmüller[94] are content to confine themselves to canon 995, § 1. Other authors elaborate on the qualities which receive express mention in the canon and explain the significance of the expression *"deque aliis iure requisitis."*

The superior must testify to the religious profession of the ordinand. In doing so he indicates whether this is temporary or perpetual, so that the status of the candidate, in relation to orders, is clear.[95] The religious superior grants a dimissorial to his subjects for all orders from the first tonsure to the priesthood,[96] but he must

88 Benedictus XIV, const. *Impositi Nobis,* 27 febr. 1747, § 5—*Fontes,* n. 376.

89 *De Sacra Ordinatione,* n. 920.

90 *De Sacra Ordinatione,* p. 430.

91 Can. 995, § 1.

92 *Enchiridion,* p. 469.

93 *Religious in Church Law* (New York: Kenedy & Sons, 1924), p. 213.

94 *Das neue Ordensrecht* (Dülmen, 1919), p. 171.

95 Cf. Fanfani, *De Iure Religiosorum,* p. 320; Schäfer, *De Religiosis,* p. 499; Cappello, *De Sacramentis,* II, Pars III, 297; Blat, *Commentarium,* III, *De Sacramentis,* 460; O'Brien, *The Exemption of Religious in Church Law,* p. 187; Biederlack († 1930)-Führich, *De Religiosis* (Oeniponte, 1919), 174.

96 Cf. can. 964.

observe certain limitations. He is forbidden to present a novice for ordination,[97] and during the triennial period preceding perpetual profession[98] he may present the candidate only for the first tonsure and the minor orders.[99] It is only after perpetual profession that the major orders may be received.[100]

In the dimissorial there also is mention of the association of the aspirant with a religious house subject to the superior issuing the letter. As already indicated, the range of competence in this regard is most extensive for the supreme moderator. Other superiors are restricted to that province or house over which they exercise authority.

How strict an interpretation is to be placed on the necessity of the candidate's being a member of a religious house subject to the grantor of the dimissorial? If the ordinand is assigned to a house but lives elsewhere, does this destroy the power of the superior of the house to which he is assigned to issue a letter for him?

Not infrequently a religious is sent to another province to pursue his studies, to obtain academic degrees, to learn another language, or for reasons of health. In these cases the dimissorial certainly may be given by the supreme moderator of the society. It seems, too, that the major superior in the province where the aspirant actually is staying, will also be able to do this. In this case the constitutions of the institute may require that he have the permission of the proper provincial of the candidate. Finally, the proper provincial may issue the dimissorial, but in doing so he directs it to the bishop in whose territory the house to which the ordinand is formally assigned is located.

It is ordinarily true that the letter is addressed to the bishop of the diocese where the house to which the religious belongs is situated.[101] In the special circumstances described in the preceding paragraph it appears that, as long as there is no semblance of fraud,[102] the

[97] Cf. can. 567, § 2.
[98] Cf. can 574.
[99] Can. 964, 3°.
[100] Can. 964, 4°.
[101] Can. 965.
[102] Can. 967.

dimissorial may be sent to either of two bishops: (1) to him in whose territory is the house with which the religious is formally connected;[103] (2) to the one within whose diocesan limits the candidate is actually residing. The major superior differs in each case if the houses are in different provinces, but in both instances the superior truly testifies that the aspirant is a member of a religious house subject to himself.

The studies to which the superior gives witness are those which are required by the general prescription for ordination. As the preceding article in this chapter indicates, the law in this matter is now the same for religious and seculars with the result that canon 976 is the governing norm for all. To give a complete picture of the learning of the candidate, the superior testifies to these studies and the examination required by canon 996.[104]

Besides these qualities expressly enumerated, other testimony is included in the dimissorial. Biederlack-Führich[105] and Goyeneche[106] understand the phrase *"deque aliis iure requisitis"* as implying reference to canon 974, § 1. They teach that the superior is obliged to include data on the confirmation, character, canonical age, requisite knowledge, reception of the preceding order, observance of the interstices, and canonical title, if it is a question of major orders. Schäfer[107] is almost as comprehensive, listing age, the last ordination, character, freedom from impediments and the retreat as necessary matter.

To the writer it appears that Biederlack-Führich, Goyeneche, and Schäfer are more stringent than the law itself. If the superior makes a general declaration that all the requirements of the Code and the constitutions of the society are satisfied, this seems to be an adequate testimonial. In this respect the superior of an exempt community enjoys greater freedom than does the superior of a nonexempt institute. In his own inquiry the superior of the exempt re-

[103] Cf. can. 587, § 4.
[104] Can. 997, § 2.
[105] *De Religiosis*, p. 174.
[106] "Consultationes," *CpR*, III (1922), 264, (2).
[107] *De Religiosis*, p. 500.

ligious investigates the fitness of the aspirant according to the norm of canon 968, § 1, the Instruction *Quantum Religiones,* and the special legislation of the particular organization. In composing his dimissorial he then needs to speak of the worthiness of the ordinand in only general terms.[108]

Over and above the demands of the Code, the decree *Quantum Religiones* instructs the religious superior to testify to the signing by the candidate both of the petition required before the profession of temporary vows and of the attestation made prior to the solemn profession and the reception of the subdiaconate.[109] It is to be noted that this and the other prescriptions of the instruction are applicable to the exempt as well as the non-exempt.[110]

3. *Adequacy of the Letter*

The second paragraph of canon 995 points to another characteristic of exemption. It declares the adequacy of the dimissorial issued by the religious superior in conformity with the first paragraph of the same canon.[111] This letter alone suffices, so that no other testimonial is required. To demand others destroys an outstanding difference between the exempt and the non-exempt. Consequently, the bishop ordaining the religious, sent to him with such a dimissorial, is assured that the prescriptions of the law are fulfilled and that the candidate is worthy of being ordained. It makes no difference who this bishop is, whether of the place where the house of the ordinand is located or one commissioned to confer orders according to the norms of canon 966, § 1. He accepts the dimissorial of the religious superior and knows that the aspirant is suitable.[112]

108 Blat, *Commentarium,* III, *De Sacramentis,* 460.

109 *Qnantum Religiones,* nn. 14, 18, 19—*AAS,* XXIV (1932), 74-81.

110 Note: Moeder details the components of the dimissorial. Both because of his treatment and also in view of the nature of the present work, these are not examined more thoroughly here. Cf. *The Proper Bishop for Ordination and Dimissorial Letters,* pp. 122-3.

111 Can. 995, § 2: Episcopus, acceptis iis litteris dimissoriis, aliis testimonialibus litteris non indiget.

112 Cf. can. 973, §§ 1, 3; Blat, *Commentarium,* III, *De Sacramentis,* 461; Goyeneche, "Consultationes," *CpR,* VIII (1927), 377.

In stating that no testimonial other than that contained in the dimissorial is necessary, the legislator clearly differentiates his demand upon the non-exempt and the exempt. Whereas the former must meet the requirements of a testimonial from the ordinaries of those places where they live long enough possibly to contract a canonical impediment[113] and from the pastor or others delegated to investigate,[114] the exempt are free from such demands. This does not mean that the suitableness of an exempt candidate is any the less certain than that of a non-exempt one. Rather, it indicates that the determination of that aptitude is dependent more on the religious superior than on those outside the institute.

Although the dimissorial of the religious superior is sufficient testimony to the worthiness of the ordinand, there occur instances when the bishop to whom the letter is sent has reason to doubt the suitableness of the candidate. If the doubt lacks a solid foundation, the bishop may proceed to ordain without fear of sharing in another's sin.[115] Even if there is positive doubt, the same course may be followed, since the religious superior is presumed to satisfy all the legal requirements relative to the preliminary investigation of the aspirant. However, if the ordaining prelate is morally certain that the candidate is unworthy he may not advance him to sacred orders.[116]

[113] Cans. 993, 4°; 994.
[114] Can. 1000, § 1.
[115] Can. 973, § 3.
[116] Can. 973, § 3. Cf. Cappello, *De Sacramentis*, II, Pars III, 297.

CHAPTER VI

EXAMINATION OF THE KNOWLEDGE OF THE ORDINAND

Article I. *Matter for the Examination*

A. *General Considerations*

The second of the scrutinies, classic in this matter, is provided for in canons 996-997. In these canons the Code consummates an evolution progressively more noticeable in the centuries since the Council of Trent. Whereas the ancient antecedents of this legislation linked the inquiry into the knowledge of the candidate with a concomitant consideration of his other qualities,[1] post-Tridentine practice separated the two. Consequently, even prior to the Code Gasparri[2] remarked that the preparatory investigation gathers all the necessary testimonies required by an examination of the candidate's fitness so that the prescribed formal examination is reduced to an exploration of the knowledge of the ordinand. The development is culminated in the Code by the recognition granted to this procedure.

Canon 996, § 1, decrees that every ordinand, secular and religious, is to be examined on the order he is to receive.[3] This applies to all aspiring to any order from the first tonsure to the priesthood. It matters not that the candidate is a secular, a religious ruled by the law of seculars, or even an exempt religious. All ordinands have a common denominator of obligation through this canon. This universality of application was a legal feature emphasized by the Tridentine declaration that even regulars were to submit to a diligent examination by the bishop, notwithstanding any privileges to the

[1] Cf. c. 5, D. XXIV—Council of Nantes, cap. XI—Mansi, XVIII a, 169; Conc. Trident., sess XXIII, *de ref.*, c. 7.

[2] *De Sacra Ordinatione*, n. 755.

[3] "Quilibet promovendus sive saecularis sive religiosus debet praevium ac diligens examen subire circa ipsum ordinem suscipiendum."

contrary.[4] Thus, a privilege in this matter, to be valid, had to be directly conceded subsequent to the Council of Trent.[5]

The examination is given prior to the reception of the order to which the candidate aspires. Certainly there is no object in deferring it until after ordination. Such a procedure defeats the very purpose of the law, viz., the determination of whether or not the ordinand has the necessary knowledge. The presence or absence of this quality is to be ascertained before ordination in order that a correct decision may be made concerning his worthiness to receive this particular order.

The examination is also characterized by the care taken in determining the knowledge possessed by the ordinand. The scrutiny is not an unimportant formality to which both examiner and examinee submit because of a whim of the legislator. To the contrary, it is an important element in the investigation preceding every ordination. Any other estimate is based on a misapprehension of the purpose and importance of the law. Consequently, the practice whereby a candidate is questioned for a few minutes on matter, either irrelevant or only accidentally pertinent to the order for which he is a candidate, is an abuse of the letter and spirit of the canon.

The matter for this examination is indicated only in a general manner in the Code. The law states that the aspirant is interrogated on the order he desires to receive. At first sight this may appear to be a relaxation of a sterner pre-Code discipline. Actually this is not the case. Although no mention is made of such specific points as a knowledge of Latin and the rudiments of the faith,[6] these are presupposed in the course of studies contemplated by the Code.[7] Because of this it is possible for the legislator in canon 996 to restrict his consideration to the material directly pertinent to the order. This is commonly understood to refer to the matter, form, minister, na-

[4] Conc. Trident., sess. XXIII, *de ref.*, c. 12.

[5] Cf. Many, *De Sacra Ordinatione*, p. 392; Blat, *Commentarium*, III, *De Sacramentis*, 462.

[6] Cf. Conc. Trident., sess. XXIII, *de ref.*, cc. 11, 4.

[7] Can. 1364, 1°, 2°. Cf. *Litterae ab Excmo Delegato Apost. ad universos Civitatum Foed. Americae Sept. ordinarios, nomine et auctoritate S.C. de Semin. et Stud. Univ. missis*, 26 mai. 1928—*Enchiridion Clericorum*, n. 1252.

ture, duties, effects and conditions of the particular order.[8] The amplifications of the following paragraphs are made on this basis. What is said concerning the various orders forms the substance of the examination, but the manuals on the subject are to be consulted for a more detailed and catechetical presentation.

B. *Minor Orders*

The candidate for tonsure particularly must demonstrate his knowledge of the effects of the step he contemplates. He must know that the reception of this order enrolls him in the clerical state[9] with certain privileges[10] and obligations.[11] He is also to understand the implication of incardination in the diocese for whose service he is promoted[12] and the aptitude imparted by tonsure for the reception of other orders, the exercise of jurisdiction and the obtaining of benefices and ecclesiastical pensions.[13] In addition he is to indicate his familiarity with the form the ordinand recites with the ordaining prelate.[14]

In common with the candidates for the other orders, the ordinand desirous of becoming a porter must understand the nature of the order to which he aspires. He is questioned on the real and nominal definitions of the term *"ostiariatus,"* and the status of this order as the first of the minors. His knowledge includes the reference the order of porter has to the people and the Holy Eucharist

[8] Cf. Cappello, *De Sacramentis,* II, Pars III, 506; Bolduc, *Les Études dans les Religions Cléricales,* p. 119.

[9] Can. 108, § 1.

[10] Cans. 119-123.

[11] Cans. 124-144.

[12] Can. 111, § 2.

[13] Can. 118.

[14] Cf. Pontificale Rom., tit. *De clerico faciendo;* Carbone, *Praxis Ordinandorum* (ed. altera, Taurini: Marietti, 1928), pp. 16-27; Roder, *Ordinandorum Enchiridion* (ed. altera curante M. Belli, Neapoli: Ex Typis Pontificiis M. D'Auria, 1928), pp. 10-4; Munerati, *Promptuarium pro Ordinandis et Confessariis Examinandis* (ed. 3, Romae, 1923), pp. 27-32; Pecorari, *Novum Manuale Ordinandorum* (2 vols., Romae: Typis Polyglottis Vaticanis, 1929), I, 118-51.

through the exercise of such duties as the opening and closing of the doors of the church, the admission of the worthy and the exclusion of the unfit, the ringing of the bells and the convoking of the people, the custody of the furnishings of the church, the opening of the book for the preacher, and, in general, the care exercised lest anything irreverent occur in the house of God.[15]

For the lectorate the aspirant is asked about this order as the second of the minor orders and as conferring the spiritual power of publicly reading the sacred books in the church and of instructing the faithful. He is to know how the lector prepares the people for the worthy reception of the Blessed Sacrament by teaching the mysteries of faith and reading the Scriptures. This candidate is also to be conversant with such duties as the reading of the lessons of the first nocturn of the divine office and the prophecies at Mass, the singing of the divine praises, and the blessing of bread and new fruits.[16]

The future exorcist knows of this as the minor order which, through the handing over of the book of exorcisms under the prescribed form, grants the spiritual power of invoking the name of God over those possessed by the devil. The ordinand also is to understand his rôle relative to the solemn expulsion of unclean spirits, the exorcism of catechumens and the preparation of the materials employed in driving out the devil. He is to know, too, the connection this order has with the Eucharist. Above all, he must realize that the exercise of this order is governed by the restrictions of canon 1151.[17]

The examination of the prospective acolyte probes his knowledge regarding the nature of the order. He is asked about the sig-

[15] Cf. Pontificale Rom., tit. *De ordinatione ostiariorum;* Carbone, *op. cit.*, pp. 44-9; Roder, *op. cit.*, pp. 31-4; Munerati, *op. cit.*, pp. 33-6; Pecorari, *op. cit.*, pp. 151-7.

[16] Can. 1147, § 4; Vermeersch-Creusen, *Epitome*, II, 284. Cf. Pontificale Rom., tit. *De ordinatione lectorum;* Carbone, *op. cit.*, pp. 49-52; Roder, *op. cit.*, pp. 35-6; Munerati, *op. cit.*, pp. 37-8; Pecorari, *op. cit.*, pp. 157-160.

[17] Cf. Pontificale Rom., tit. *De ordinatione exorcistorum;* Carbone, *op. cit.*, pp. 52-7; Roder, *op. cit.*, pp. 37-8; Munerati, *op. cit.*, pp. 39-41; Pecorari, *op. cit.*, pp. 171-7.

nificance of the unlighted candle and empty cruets given him by the bishop. He also must be familiar with the duties of preparing the wine and water for the celebration of Mass and of offering them to the subdeacon, of lighting the candles and of carrying them during the Holy Sacrifice, of serving the deacon and the subdeacon at the altar, of carrying the thurible and of serving private Masses. Finally, he must know the conditions under which the acolyte may act as a subdeacon at solemn Mass.[18]

C. *Major Orders*

Besides the general matter indicated above, the candidate for the subdiaconate is questioned on the significance of being given the chalice, paten and book of epistles and their use at solemn Mass. Familiarity with the particular obligations assumed by the subdeacon relative to the recitation of the divine office and the observance of chastity is also tested.[19]

In the examination preliminary to the reception of the diaconate, there is questioning on the nature and exercise of the spiritual power of immediately assisting the priest in his sacred functions. Moreover, the candidate is to have cognizance of the conditions under which the deacon may preach,[20] bless,[21] expose the Blessed Sacrament,[22] administer solemn baptism,[23] and distribute Holy Communion.[24]

When examined for the priesthood the ordinand must appreciate the sacerdotal power over the real and mystical body of Christ.

[18] Cf. Pontificale Rom., tit. *De ordinatione acolythorum;* Carbone, *Praxis,* pp. 58-63; Roder, *Enchiridion,* pp. 39-41; Munerati, *Promptuarium,* pp. 42-4; Pecorari, *Manuale,* pp. 177-80.

[19] Cf. Pontificale Rom., tit. *De ordinatione subdiaconi;* Carbone, *op. cit.,* pp. 80-108; Roder, *op. cit.,* pp. 57-66; Munerati, *op. cit.,* pp. 45-57; Pecorari, *op. cit.,* pp. 182-207.

[20] Can. 1342, § 1.

[21] Can. 1147, § 4.

[22] Can. 1274, § 2.

[23] Can. 741.

[24] Can.. 845, § 2. Cf. Carbone, *Praxis,* pp. 110-5; Roder, *Enchiridion,* pp. 67-70; Munerati, *Promptuarium,* pp. 58-65; Pecorari, *Manuale,* I, 207-58.

He is interrogated concerning the matter and form of Holy Orders, the proper consecration and administration of the sacraments, and the instruction of the people. To satisfy this demand, the knowledge of the aspirant includes an understanding of the requisites for offering sacrifice and of such allied subjects as the doctrine of the Eucharist, the value and fruit of the Mass, its rites and ceremonies, the time and place for celebration, the requirements in the celebrant, and the law on stipends. Then, too, he is to demonstrate his knowledge of other powers of the priest, such as those of blessing, presiding and preaching.[25]

Besides the examination on the nature, effect, matter, form, minister, etc., the candidate for sacred orders is also questioned on other tracts in sacred theology.[26] Aspirants to the subdiaconate, diaconate, and priesthood are liable for relatively more than ordinands seeking advancement to the minor orders. Prior to the Code there was emphasis on knowledge of moral theology,[27] but the addition of a theological tract for the examination on the major orders is new as general legislation. Former law included certain norms in this regard, but the pre-Code prescriptions had particular application, e.g., in Italy[28] and in the diocese of Westminster.[29]

Canon 996, § 2, speaks of tracts in sacred theology without any precise determination of what is meant. Goyeneche[30] and Bolduc[31] point out that "theology" has various significations in the Code.[32] In the present case, although an obligation is imposed, it appears that

[25] Cf. Innocentius XIII, const. *Apostolici ministerii,* 23 maii 1723, § 5—*Fontes,* n. 280; Pontificale Rom., tit. *De ordinatione presbyteri;* Carbone, *op. cit.,* pp. 136-225; Roder, *op. cit.,* pp. 71-84; Munerati, *op. cit.,* pp. 66-89; Pecorari, *op. cit.,* pp. 258-475.

[26] Can. 996, § 3: Promovendi vero ad sacros ordines in aliis quoque de sacra theologia tractationibus periculum faciant.

[27] Innocentius XIII, *loc. cit.*

[28] Pius X, motu propr. *Religiosorum Ordinum,* 19 mart. 1906—*Fontes,* n. 673.

[29] I Provincial Council of Westminster (1852), tit. XXI—*Collectio Lacensis,* III, 936.

[30] "Consultationes," *CpRM,* XIX (1938), 84.

[31] *Les Études dans les Religions Cléricales,* p. 120.

[32] Cf. cans. 589, § 1; 590; 1366, §§ 2, 3, etc.

there is to be a broad understanding of the term. Thus, strictly theological tracts such as those *De Deo Trino, De Verbo Incarnato, De gratia Christi,* may be designated, but other matter, outside the precise limits of dogma and moral, may be inserted.[33] This interpretation has a pre-Code basis in the general demands of Innocent XIII (1721-1724)[34] and the post-Code declaration admitting the possibility of inclusion in this examination of matter on which a candidate for a pastorate is interrogated.[35]

Canon 996, §§ 1, 2, determines the necessary material for this examination. The third paragraph of the same canon expresses the option enjoyed by the bishop in deciding on the tract in sacred theology.[36] It is fitting that he do this for, more than anybody else, the bishop is conversant with the end to be achieved by the test. In the United States, where active ministerial work is usually undertaken immediately after ordination, it is advisable to designate tracts directly pertinent to this activity. Thus, the sacramental tracts on marriage, baptism and penance may be successively chosen for the three major orders. Certainly these are covered in the course of theology, but they may be emphasized and reviewed by insertion in the examination for sacred orders.

Article II. *Mode of Examination and Selection of Examiners*

As the determination of the tracts in sacred theology pertains to the bishop, so also does the manner of inquiry and the selection of the examiners. The examination is oral or written, dependent on

[33] Cf. Cappello, *De Sacramentis,* II, Pars III, 506.

[34] *Loc. cit.*

[35] PCI, 24 nov. 1920—*AAS,* XII (1920), 574.

Note: A decree of the Sacred Congregation for the Oriental Church, 27 Jan. 1940, establishes the following norm for its subjects: In examine coram Commissione subeundo unusquisque candidatus satisfacere debet: 1) de sua ipsius praeparatione morali et ascetica; 2) de scientia practica atque theologica cuiusvis Ordinis suscipiendi; 3) de institutione doctrinali, inspectis in primis theologia dogmatica, morali et sacramentaria, liturgia et iure canonico. —*AAS,* XXXII (1940), 156.

[36] Can. 996, § 3: Episcoporum est statuere . . . quibus in tractationibus sacrae theologiae promovendi periculum facere debeant.

what he decides, but, whatever the mode, Latin is the medium to be employed. Although this is not expressly stated in general legislation, the mind of the Holy See is clear from its attitude toward this language.[37] For the United States there is expression of this intention in the letter sent to the ordinaries of this country by the Apostolic Delegate at the instigation of the Sacred Congregation of Seminaries and Universities. This communication states that "all examinations, and especially those which students are required to take before being admitted to Sacred Orders, must be held in Latin."[38]

The margin permitted in the satisfaction of the accidentals of this legislation is further emphasized by the absence of any indication as to the number of these examinations. As long as the required matter is covered, any reasonable combination is acceptable. Thus, there is no objection to one examination for the first tonsure and the minor orders and another for the majors.[39] Certainly there is no need to maintain, as Raus[40] does, that two examinations, one on the order and the other on the theological tract, are necessary before the reception of the subdiaconate and of other sacred orders. A normal course follows the observance of the interstices, so that a separate interrogation for each of the major orders is a logical procedure. However, in the absence of express provision in the matter, it suffices that there be an examination and that the prescribed material be included.

Relative freedom is also enjoyed in the choice of examiners. The bishop himself may conduct the examination or he may employ others who are delegated for this purpose. In making his selection he is obliged only by the necessity of choosing capable men. As long as this is done, there is no legal demand that any official, individual or group be designated. Canon 389, § 2, explicitly ratifies this pro-

[37] Cf. S.C. de Sem. et Stud. Univ., litt. *Vixdum haec Sacra Congregatio*, 9 oct. 1921, III A—*Enchiridion Clericorum*, n. 1125; Pius XI, ep. ap. *Officiorum omnium*, 1 aug. 1922—*ibid.*, n. 1154; Pius XI, ep. ap. *Unigenitus Dei Filius*, 19 mart. 1924—*ibid.*, n. 1189.

[38] 26 mai. 1928—*Enchiridion Clericorum*, n. 1253.

[39] Cf. Cappello, *Summa*, II, 459.

[40] *Institutiones*, p. 100.

cedure by decreeing that, for the reception of orders, the bishop may employ the synodal examiners or others.[41] In the majority of cases the most convenient and satisfactory arrangement is for the bishop to designate the faculty of the seminary or the religious superiors to examine the candidates.[42]

Article III. *Right to Examine*

A. *Local Ordinary*

Canon 997, § 1, expressly declares that the local ordinary who by right ordains or grants a dimissorial letter controls the examination.[43] Granted the possession of the necessary power of orders, this ordinary is determined as the proper conferrer of orders by canons 956, 957 and 965, and as the conceder of the dimissorial by canon 958. Excluded from consideration here are the major religious superiors referred to in canon 964. They are not local ordinaries.[44]

This power of the local ordinary extends to both seculars and religious candidates, or, in other words, to the ordinands included in the considerations of canon 993. Thus, seculars and those religious who are governed by the law of seculars are obliged to submit to the examination controlled by the local ordinary who by right ordains or grants them a dimissorial.

For a just cause the local ordinary may commission the ordaining bishop to undertake the task of examining if the latter is willing to comply with the request. From this it is clear that the usual procedure demands that the examination be undertaken by the one who has the right to ordain or who by law is entitled to grant the dimissorial.[45] Even if a bishop is given a letter empowering him to or-

41 "Pro experimentis vero habendis ad clericorum ordinationem . . . integrum est Episcopo vel examinatorum synodalium vel aliorum opera uti."

42 Raus, *loc. cit.;* Fanfani, *De Iure Religiosorum,* p. 323; Schäfer, *Re Religiosis,* p. 501; Pejska, *Ius Canonicum Religiosorum* (ed. 3, Friburgi Brisgoviae: Herder, 1927), p. 310.

43 "Hoc examen sive pro clericis saecularibus sive pro religiosis recipit loci Ordinarius qui iure proprio ordinat, aut dat dimissorias litteras; qui tamen potest quoque, ex iusta causa, illud Episcopo ordinaturo committere, qui id oneris suscipere velit."

44 Cf. can. 198, § 2.

45 Cappello, *De Sacramentis,* II, Pars III, 507; Wernz-Vidal, *Ius Can-*

dain a subject of this proper ordinary, the ordinary himself examines. However, if there is a just case, e.g., if the ordinand is studying at the seminary of the ordaining bishop, this bishop may be delegated to test the knowledge of the candidate. In such a case the proper ordinary does not divest himself of responsibility merely by sending a dimissorial delegating another to ordain.[46] The bishop who is to impose hands must accept the burden. If he does so, there is no particular difficulty; should he refuse to examine, it devolves upon the proper ordinary to question the aspirant, commission another who is competent, or address the dimissorial to a bishop who is willing to examine.

B. *Ordaining Bishop*

The distinction between the local ordinary and the ordaining bishop is of importance. Frequently they are one and the same person, but in virtue of canon 955, § 1, and canon 966, § 1, it is not unusual to have different prelates in the two rôles. In any event, the power to examine, if it be exercised by the bishop delegated to ordain, is referrible to his imposition of hands and not to any territorial consideration. This is in complete accord with the status of this bishop as outlined in canon 973, § 3, and is particularly true when he elevates a candidate to major orders. In these cases he must be morally certain of the worthiness of the recipient.

In canon 997, § 2, it is supposed that the bishop is ordaining a candidate who is not his own subject. Moreover, there is no question of an examination being requested by the superior of the ordinand. When presented to the minister of the sacrament the aspirant is provided with a dimissorial attesting to the completion of the examination and declaring him worthy of ordination.[47]

onicum, tom. IV, *De Rebus,* I, 362.

[46] Blat, *Commentarium,* III, *De Sacramentis,* 464.

[47] Can. 997, § 2: Episcopus alienum subditum sive saecularem sive religiosum ordinans cum legitimis litteris dimissoriis, quibus asseritur candidatum examinatum fuisse ad normam § 1, et idoneum repertum, potest huic attestationi acquiescere, sed non tenetur; et si pro sua conscientia censeat candidatum non esse idoneum, eum ne promoveat.

On receipt of the dimissorial the ordaining bishop may accept its assurances. However he is not obliged to do so.[48] If there is question of major orders and he is not morally certain of the worthiness of the aspirant[49] this bishop may not advance the candidate before satisfying his own conscience. When this situation arises the ordaining bishop may require a re-examination.

May the ordaining bishop, on his own initiative, examine the ordinand, or must he be delegated for this purpose by the proper ordinary? The answer to this question is by no means certain. Canon 997, § 2, itself is obscure on the point. However, it is true that the law is not an innovation introduced with the Code. It has antecedents, particularly in the replies of the Sacred Congregation of the Council. In these statements there was an expression of the right of the ordaining bishop to examine under the conditions currently set forth in canon 997, § 2.[50] Precisely because of the resultant presumption of identity between the canon and its antecedents, it is the opinion of the writer that the ordaining bishop may examine of his own accord.

C. *Superior of the Exempt Religious*

The Code speaks of a local ordinary possessing the right to ordain and, as a consequence, to examine. Considered in itself and without reference to the second part of canon 997, this declaration seems to make canon 997, § 1, applicable to all religious without distinction. Apparently this is the understanding of Fanfani when he writes without qualification that religious ordinands are totally dependent on the local bishop in this regard.[51] Such a consideration is based on the fact that even the exempt have a proper bishop to whom the necessary letters are sent.[52] However, in canon 997, § 2, it is asserted that a bishop ordaining the subject of another, secular

[48] *Quantum Religiones,* n. 12—*AAS,* XXIV (1932), 78; Biederlack-Führich, *De Religiosis,* p. 175; Vermeersch-Creusen, *Epitome,* II, 167; Bouuaert-Simenon, *Manuale,* II, 191.

[49] Can. 973, § 3.

[50] Cf. S.C.C., *Mileten.,* 20 nov. 1592—*Fontes,* n. 2252; *Nullius,* 16 ian. 1593—*Fontes,* n. 2253; 17 ian. 1693—*Fontes,* n. 2934.

[51] *De Iure Religiosorum,* p. 322.

[52] Can. 965.

or religious, with a dimissorial stating that the candidate is examined and judged worthy may be satisfied with this attestation.

The problem is the old one of relationship between the local ordinary and exempt religious. These religious have a local ordinary, but only in the tenuous sense that the dimissorial is sent to the ordinary of the place where the religious house is situated. It is also true that they are withdrawn from the jurisdiction of this bishop.[53] The consequence of this is that the local ordinary, in imposing hands on these religious, is ordaining the subjects of another. The question that arises from this procedure concerns the relative rights of the local ordinary and the religious superior over the examination.

In pre-Code legislation there is frequent reference to an examination of regulars by the bishop. Much of this is indefinite because of the failure to specify which bishop, the ordaining prelate or the local ordinary possessing the right to ordain, is to examine.[54] On the other hand, there are several documents in which there is precise mention of a doctrinal examination of regulars by the ordaining bishop.[55] If it be supposed that the obscure citations are to be understood in conformity with the explicit enunciations, it may be stated that prior to the Code the right to examine belonged to the ordaining bishop, and not to the ordinary of the place where the religious house was situated.

Since the current legislation is presumed to be identical with the earlier law,[56] it seems that regulars may now be examined by the ordaining bishop, but that a local ordinary, as such, does not possess this right.

The wording of the Code itself supports this contention. There is no doubt of the ability of exempt religious superiors to grant a dimissorial for their subjects.[57] In this letter it is necessary that

[53] Cf. can. 615.

[54] Cf. Conc. Trident., sess. XXIII, *de ref.*, c. 12; Innocentius XIII, const. *Apostolici ministerii*, 23 maii 1723, § 5—*Fontes*, n. 280; Benedictus XIII, const. *In supremo*, 23 sept. 1724, § 4—*Fontes*, n. 283.

[55] Benedictus XIV, const. *Impositi Nobis*, 27 febr. 1747, § 4—*Fontes*, n. 376; S.C.C., decr. 15 mart. 1596—*Fontes*, n. 2294.

[56] Can. 6, 4°.

[57] Can. 965.

there be included an attestation to the effect that the candidate is considered worthy because of a judgment based on this examination.[58] The logical consequence of this obligation is the admission of the right of the religious superior to examine.[59] The exercise of this right excludes the ordinary of the place where the religious house is located when this ordinary does not ordain.

When the local ordinary is not the minister for orders his function is restricted to the concession of the letter which permits another bishop to ordain.[60] This, too, is in complete accord with the status of the exempt. Instead of the local ordinary inquiring into the fitness of the candidate, the complete investigation is performed by the superiors of the institute. These superiors have the means necessary for a thorough examination of the aspirant, and their obligations and rights parallel those exercised by a local ordinary over his own subjects.[61] In both cases the only restriction imposed is in favor of the ordaining bishop. If anything, the exempt religious superior enjoys greater freedom since his subjects do not need to present the testimonials of canon 993, 4°, whereas the candidate obliged to the law of seculars may be asked by the ordaining bishop not only for these but for more precise testimonials.[62]

Some religious institutes, notably the Society of Jesus,[63] enjoy the privilege whereby their subjects are excused from an examination by the ordaining bishop. Because of the provision of the Council of Trent[64] it is necessary that such a privilege be granted subsequently to this Council. A concession of this kind is still operative in virtue of can 4.

[58] Can. 997, § 2. Cf. can. 995, § 1.

[59] Cf. Cappello, *De Sacramentis,* II, Pars III, 507; O'Brien, *The Exemption of Religious in Church Law,* p. 188; Arregui, *Summarium Theologiae Moralis* (ed. 13, Romae: Deposito Libri della Pont. Università Gregoriana, 1937), p. 486.

[60] Cf. can. 966, § 1.

[61] *Quantum Religiones,* n. 12—*AAS,* XXIV (1932), 78.

[62] Can. 994, § 1.

[63] Gregorius XIII, const. *Pium et utile,* 22 sept. 1582—*Bullarum Diplomatum et Privilegiorum Sanctorum Pontificum,* VIII, 397.

[64] Sess. XXIII, *de ref.,* c. 12.

CHAPTER VII

DELICTS IN THE EXAMINATION OF ORDINANDS

Article I. *Administration of Orders*

Prior to the reception of orders seculars and those who are governed by the law of seculars are to produce certain testimonials. The law enjoins that they are not to be ordained without these letters. Violators of the prohibition are suspended *ipso facto* for a year from the conferring of orders, and the dispensation from the penalty is reserved to the Apostolic See.[1]

This sanction is a reiteration almost verbatim, of the penalty determined for the same offense in the Constitution *Apostolicae Sedis.*[2] From its wording several facts are immediately apparent. First of all, it is effective only when testimonial letters are required and they are not produced. Consequently there is no question of this penalty being incurred when the ordinand is an exempt religious. Such a candidate does not need the letters demanded by canon 993, 4°, and 994. However, for the non-exempt canon 2373, 2°, is pertinent in that they must secure these testimonials. Since no reference is made to the letter of the major superior,[3] the sanction is not incurred if this testimonial is not provided.[4]

To fall into the suspension the minister must be delinquent in the ordination of his own subject. If a candidate is sent to a bishop with the necessary dimissorial, this bishop may proceed to ordain and

[1] Can. 2373: In suspensionem per annum ab ordinum collatione Sedi Apostolicae reservatam ipso facto incurrunt: 2°. Qui subditum proprium, qui alibi tanto tempore moratus sit ut canonicum impedimentum contrahere ibi poterit, ordinaverint contra praescriptum can. 993, n. 4, 994.

[2] Pius IX, 12 oct. 1869, § V, n. 3—*Fontes,* n. 552.

[3] Can. 993, 5°.

[4] Cf. can. 19.

yet fail to incur the suspension even though he knows that one or the other of the testimonials is lacking. The reason is that the bishop imposes hands on the subject of another. Under these same circumstances the one issuing the dimissorial also seems to escape suspension since he is not the actual minister for ordination.[5]

In ordaining his own subject the bishop needs the testimonials mentioned in canons 993, 4° and 994. These letters are the ones required of an ordinand who spends six months in a place on attaining puberty or, in the case of a soldier, if he is there for half that time. Because of the possibility that a canonical impediment may be contracted during this residence, the bishop must have these testimonials before he imposes hands. Failure to observe this law results in the suspension of the minister for ordination.

If episcopal prudence indicates a need for testimonials to cover a shorter period or for a time prior to puberty, these are to be obtained; but if they are nevertheless not obtained, the suspension is not incurred. The penalty is attached only to that to which the law obliges the ordaining ordinary.

In the event that a local ordinary does not know enough about the aspirant to grant a testimonial, or if the procurement of all the necessary letters is impossible or too difficult, a suppletory oath is to be taken by the candidate. If the bishop ordains without regard for this provision he is *ipso facto* suspended. This is true because this oath is considered equivalent to a testimonial, and canon 2373, 2°, refers to canon 994 in its entirety, and not merely to one or the other of its paragraphs.

The suspension is incurred immediately upon the violation of the law. As the use of the phrase "*ipso facto*" indicates, this penalty is in the category of those which are classified as *latae sententiae*

[5] Cf. Chelodi, *Ius Poenale* (Tridenti: Libr. Edit. Tridentum, 1925 [1920?]), 126; Cappello, *Tractatus Canonico-Moralis de Censuris* (ed. altera, Taurinorum Augustae: Marietti, 1925), p. 461; Ayrinhac, *Penal Legislation in the New Code of Canon Law* (revised by Lydon, New York: Benziger, 1936), p. 284; Sipos, *Enchiridion,* p. 469; Beste, *Introductio,* p. 966; Murphy, *Delinquencies and Penalties in the Administration and Reception of the Sacraments,* The Catholic University of America Canon Law Studies, n. 17 (Washington, D. C.: The Catholic University of America, 1923), p. 96.

penalties.[6] Upon the completion of the delict—in this case ordination without the required testimonials—the minister is suspended.[7] Ignorance of the law or of the penalty alone, even if not crass, does not excuse the ordaining prelate because this is a *poena vindicativa latae sententiae.*[8] Only "venially culpable ignorance exempts from the incurring of vindicative penalties when the sanction of the law does not presuppose perfect *dolus.*"[9] It is required only that the minister know that there is a penalty attached to his mode of action.[10]

Despite the unsupported contention of Blat[11] to the contrary, this particular suspension is a vindicative penalty.[12] Its primary purpose is punishment for the fault. Reformation of the delinquent is a secondary consideration. As a consequence, the remission of this penalty is not warranted by the recession from contumacy on the part of the offender. Instead, the culpable party remains suspended for the definite period of a year unless a dispensation is obtained from the Holy See.

Since this is a vindicative penalty incurred *ipso facto,* it begins to bind immediately upon the commission of the delict. The illegal ordination is itself the starting point for computing the year of suspension. Because of this, it seems that the time is reckoned according to canon 34, § 3, 2°. Under this mode of computation the first day, that on which the crime is committeed, is not counted, and the suspension ceases on the completion of the last day bearing the same date a year later. Thus, a suspension incurred on January 20, 1944, lapses at midnight of January 20-21, 1945. However, in this case it

6 Can. 2217, § 2: Poena intelligitur semper ferendae sententiae, nisi expresse dicatur eam esse *latae sententiae* vel *ipso facto* seu *ipso iure* contrahi, vel nisi alia similia verba adhibeantur.

7 Cf. can. 2228.

8 Can. 2229, § 3, 1°.

9 Swoboda, *Ignorance iin Relation to the Imputability of Delicts,* The Catholic University of America Canon Law Studies, n. 143 (Washington, D. C.: The Catholic University of America Press, 1941), p. 224. Cf. can. 2218, § 2.

10 Cf. can, 2202, § 2.

11 *Commentarium,* VI, 289.

12 Cf. can. 2298, 2°.

also seems permissible to employ, as Blat[13] does, a reckoning from moment to moment, in view of the example used in canon 34, § 2.[14]

Article II. *Reception of Orders*

In the event that the examination of the qualities of a cleric fails to establish his worthiness, the superior has an obligation not to promote him to orders. This holds true although the commission of a delict is only probable, or also when a penal action against a delict certainly committed can no longer be resorted to in view of the total lapse of time during which a judicial redress was made possible.[15]

Here there is question not of coactive but of administrative power. It may happen that a candidate for orders, whose worthiness is not apparent, is probably guilty of a crime, but proof sufficient to establish his culpability is lacking. Or, if this same type of candidate is certainly guilty, penal action against him is impossible because of the lapse of time during which an accusation could have been entered in court.[16] In both these instances the superior is obliged not to promote him. He himself is not to impose hands, nor is he to grant a dimissorial enabling another to do so.

Coronata[17] points out that, in applying canon 2222, § 2, to a cleric two elements are required: (1) his worthiness is not demonstrated and (2) he is probably, but not certainly, guilty of a delict, or he is certainly guilty but penal action is precluded by the agency of legal prescription. In the case of a candidate for the first tonsure the first of these elements alone suffices to forbid his reception of orders. Additional consideration is due aspirants to the other orders since they have already entered the clerical state with the intention

[13] *Commentarium*, VI, 289.

[14] Cf. Dubé, *The General Principles for the Reckoning of Time in Canon Law*, p. 217.

[15] Can. 2222, § 2: Pariter idem legitimus Superior, licet probabile tantum sit delictum fuisse commissum aut delicti certe commissi poenalis actio praescripta sit, non solum ius, sed etiam officium habet non promovendi clericum de cuius idoneitate non constat. . . Cf. can. 970.

[16] Cf. cans. 1702-1703.

[17] *Institutiones*, IV, 88.

of advancing further[18] and a prohibition against this step is more serious for him than for a laic.

Besides the general provision for action on the part of the superior, the Code also legislates for the fault of the ordinand who undertakes to receive orders without a dimissorial or with a falsified one. The penalty for this is *ipso facto* incurred suspension from the exercise of the order received.[19]

The sanction is of a *latae sententiae* character and immediately deprives the subject affected of the use of the order he illegally obtains.[20] It is effective in the case of all orders with the exception of the first tonsure, which of course confers no power of orders in relation to which suspension could become operative.

The penalty may be incurred through ordination without a dimissorial. A candidate, examined or not, presents himself to a bishop and is ordained despite the lack of this letter. The result is that the ordained is *ipso facto* suspended from the order received, and the prelate imposing hands is suspended in a similar manner from the conferring of orders for a year.[21] The two penalties differ in that the sanction inflicted on the subject of orders is a censure reserved to no one, while the minister is afflicted with a vindicative penalty reserved to the Apostolic See.[22]

For the falsification of a dimissorial the sanction is the same as for the culpable lack of its being presented. Ordinarily, changes made in the content of the letter are not of benefit to an ordinand, since the letter is not issued unless he is thought worthy of ordination. If, for some reason, there is a substantial alteration for which the candidate is liable, the suspension is incurred.

18 Can. 973, § 1.

19 Can. 2374: Qui sine litteris vel cum falsis dimissoriis . . . ad ordines malitiose accesserit, est ipso facto a recepto ordine suspensus; qui autem sine litteris testimonialibus vel detentus aliqua censura, irregularitate, aliove impedimento, gravibus poenis secundum rerum adiuncta puniatur.

20 Cf. can. 2279, § 2, 5°.

21 Can. 2373, 1°.

22 Note: For the sanctions applicable to Orientals in the commission of similar delicts cf. S.C. pro Eccl. Orient., decr. 27 ian. 1940—*AAS,* XXXII (1940), 156.

A more likely falsification is that which results from the lack of truth in the content of the dimissorial. Although granted by a qualified authority, one or more of the attestations may not conform to the truth. In this case, as when the letter is completely lacking in authenticity, the aspirant is suspended if he is perfectly culpable.

The last half of canon 2374 provides for the punishment of a candidate who undertakes to receive ordination without testimonials, or while he is bound by a censure, an irregularity or some other impediment. In contrast to the first part of the canon, this latter penalty is of a *ferendae sententiae* character and lacks precise determination.[23] Yet it is an offense that is serious and therefore is to be punished as circumstances dictate.[24]

The sanction may result from failure to produce the letters demanded by canon 993, 4°, 5°. It is noteworthy that this part of canon 2374 makes no mention of a false testimonial. Because of this it seems that the use of such a letter is not punishable under this canon. However, the sanction of canon 2362 is applicable.

If testimonials are unobtainable, the aspirant is ordained only after supplying for this deficiency by an oath. Should he affirm under this oath what he knows to be false, he commits perjury and is punished as the prudence of the ordinary commands.[25]

Actually, to be subject to either part of canon 2374, it is necessary that there be perfect *dolus*. The use of the word "*malitiose*" in the canon indicates this. Any diminution of culpability, either on the part of the intellect or on the side of the will, excuses the ordinand.[26]

[23] Cf. can. 2217, 1, 1°

[24] Cf. can. 2223, § 3.

[25] Can. 2323: Qui blasphemaverit vel periurium extra iudicium commiserit, prudenti Ordinarii arbitrio puniatur, maxime clericus.

[26] Can. 2229, § 2. Cf. Chelodi, *Ius Poenale*, p. 128; Coronata, *Institutiones*, IV, 615; Swoboda, *Ignorance in Relation to the Imputability of Delicts*, pp. 97-9.

CONCLUSIONS

The following are the conclusions reached as a result of this study:

1. Prior to the Council of Trent a formal examination of the ordinand was not necessary since approval by the people was considered sufficient.

2. The candidate has the fundamental obligation of demonstrating his worthiness to be ordained and must gather the testimonials and attestations necessary for this purpose.

3. In the absence of the ordinary *testimonium* for baptism or ordination, the oath of the ordinand may be unacceptable as complete proof of the reception of the sacrament.

5. No *testimonium* to studies is required for the minor orders other than first tonsure.

6. It is probable that *canonicum impedimentum* of canons 993-1000 refers not only to the irregularities and simple impediments of canons 984, 985 and 987, but also to whatever in the candidate is incongruous with the clerical state.

7. The three or six months determining a need for a testimonial because of the possibility of contracted impediments, are computed morally, so that there is an approximation to the physical reckoning.

8. *Pro militibus* of canon 994, § 1, now refers to all those in the armed forces and not merely to clerics in such service.

9. Besides the ordaining bishop, the proper ordinary, when not the actual minister of ordination, may avail himself of the exceptional provisions of canon 994, § 1.

10. Even when there is moral certainty that the ordinand is unhampered by a canonical impediment, the testimonials are to be obtained.

11. If one or another testimonial is impossible or too difficult to obtain, the obligation remains to acquire such other testimonials as are obtainable.

12. The impending reception of sacred orders is announced in every parish church of the candidate.

13. The pastor is competent to change the announcement of ordination from a day of precept and to a service other than the Holy Sacrifice.

14. Unlike the banns of marriage, an ordinary may dispense with the publication of ordination only within his own territory.

15. For non-exempt religious the attestations and testimonials of canon 993 are forwarded to the ordinary with the right to ordain or grant a dimissorial.

16. The testimonials granted by a local ordinary to a candidate for entrance into a religious institute are unacceptable for ordination unless they satisfy the temporal demands of canon 994 and are granted with a view to the reception of orders.

17. Independently of any course the ordaining bishop may pursue, the proper ordinary has the primary obligation of examining the knowledge of his own subject.

18. The ordaining bishop may of his own accord undertake a doctrinal examination of a candidate presenting a dimissorial attesting to his worthiness.

19. The superior of exempt religious has the right to examine his own subjects but the ordaining bishop may also examine them if he so desires.

20. The sanction of canon 2373, 2°, is not applicable to exempt religious.

BIBLIOGRAPHY

SOURCES

Acta Apostolicae Sedis, Commentarium Officiale, Romae, 1909—

Acta Conciliorum et Epistolae Decretales ac Constitutiones Summorum Pontificum, ed. Regia, 10 vols., Parisiis, 1714-1715.

Acta et Decreta Concilii Plenarii Americae Latinae in Urbe Celebrati, A.D. MDCCCXCIX, 2 vols., Romae, 1902-1910.

Acta et Decreta Concilii Plenarii Baltimorensis Tertii, A.D. MDCCLXXXIV, Baltimorae, 1886.

Acta et Decreta Sacrorum Conciliorum Recentiorum, Collectio Lacensis, 7 vols., Friburgi Brisgoviae, 1870-1890.

Acta Sanctae Sedis, 41 vols., Romae, 1865-1908.

Bullarum Diplomatum et Privilegiorum Sanctorum Pontificum Taurinensis Editio, 24 vols., Augustae Taurinorum, 1857-1872.

Codex Iuris Canonici Pii X Pontificis Maximi iussu digestus Benedicti Papae XV auctoritate promulgatus, Rome, 1918.

Codex Iustinianus, recensivit Paulus Krueger, Berolini, 1877.

Codicis Iuris Canonici Fontes cura Emi Petri Card. Gasparri editi, 9 vols., Romae (postea Civitate Vaticana): Typis Polyglottis Vaticanis, 1923-1939. Vols. VII-IX ed. *cura et studio Emi Iustiniani Card. Serédi.*

Collectanea in Usum Secretariae Sacrae Congregationis Episcoporum et Regularium, cura A. Bizzarri, Romae, 1885.

Collectanea S. Congregationis de Propaganda Fide, 2 vols., Romae, 1907.

Collectanea S. Congregationis de Propaganda Fide seu Decreta, Instructiones, Rescripta pro Apostolicis Missionibus ex Tabulario eiusdem Sacrae Congregationis Deprompta, Romae, 1893.

Concilii Plenarii Baltimorensis II, in Ecclesia Metropolitana Baltimorensi, a die VII ad diem XXI Octobris, A.D. MDCCCLXVI, Habiti, et a Sede Apostolica Recogniti, Acta et Decreta, Baltimorae, 1868.

Corpus Iuris Canonici, Editio Lipsiensis II (Friedberg), 2 vols., Lipsiae, 1879-1881. Editio anastice repetita, 1922.

Decretales D. Gregorii Papae IX suae integritati una cum glossis restitutae, ad exemplar Romanum diligenter recognitae, Venetiis, 1591.

Decretum Gratiani emendatum et notationibus illustratum una cum glossis, Gregorio XIII, Pont. Max., iussu editum, 2 vols., Venetiis, 1591.

Enchiridion Clericorum, Documenta Ecclesiae Sacrorum Alumnis Instituendis, Romae: Typis Polyglottis Vaticanis, 1938.

Jaffé, P., *Regesta Pontificum Romanorum ab condita Ecclesia ad annum post Christum natum, 1198, Editionem secundam correctam et auctam auspiciis Gulielmi Wattenbach curaverunt S. Loewenfeld, F. Kaltenbrunner, P. Ewald,* 2 vols. in 1, Lipsisae, 1885-1888.

Liber Sextus Decretalium D. Bonifacii Papae VIII, Clementis Papae V Constitutiones, Extravagantes tum Virginti D. Ioannis Papae XXII tum Communes. Haec omnia cum suis glossis integritati restituta, & ad exemplar Romanum diligenter recognita, Venetiis, 1591.

Mansi, I. D., *Sacrorum Conciliorum Nova et Amplissima Collectio,* 53 vols. in 59, Paris, Leipzig, Arnhem, 1901-1927.

Monumenta Germaniae Historica, Gregorii I Papae Registrum Epistolarum, 4 vols., ed. L. M. Hartmann post Pauli Ewaldi obitum, Berolini, 1887-1899.

———, *Legum Sectio II: Capitularia Regum Francorum,* Tom. I, ed. A. Boretius, Hannoverae, 1883.

Novum Testamentum, Textus Latinus ex Vulgata Versione Sixti V, P.M., iussu recognita et Clementis VIII, P.M., auctoritate edita repetitus, ed. 15, Lipsiae, 1907.

Pontificale Romanum Summorum Pontificum iussu editum et a Benedicto XIV, Pont. Max., recognitum et castigatum, 3 vols., Romae, 1848.

Potthast, A., *Regesta Pontificum Romanorum inde ab anno post Christum natum 1198 ad annum 1304,* 2 vols., Berolini, 1874-1875.

Quinque Compilationes Antiquae, ed. Friedberg, Lipsiae, 1882.

Schroeder, H., *Canons and Decrees of the Council of Trent,* St. Louis: Herder, 1941.

Synodus Dioecesana Fargensis Prima, A.D. 1941 habita, Milwaukee: Bruce, 1941.

Thesaurus Resolutionum Sacrae Congregationis Concilii, 167 vols., Romae, 1718-1908.

AUTHORS

Aertnys, J.-Damen, C., *Theologia Moralis,* ed. 12, 2 vols., Taurinorum Augustae: Marietti, 1932.

Aguilar, M., *Institutiones Iuris Canonici,* ed. altera, Santo Domingo de la Calgada, 1904.

Alphonsus Maria De Ligorio, S., *Theologia Moralis,* ed. absolutissima, 9 vols., Vesontione, 1832.

Antonius a Sancto Joseph-Nicolaus a Pmo. Corde Mariae, *Compendium Salmanticense,* ed. 8, 2 vols., Burgis: Tipographia "El Monte Carmelo," 1931.

Arregui, A., *Summarium Theologiae Moralis,* ed. 13, Romae: Deposito Libri della Pont. Università Gregoriana, 1937.

Ayrinhac, H., *Constitution of the Church in the New Code of Canon Law*, New York: Benziger, 1925.

———, *Legislation on the Sacraments in the New Code of Canon Law*, New York: Longmans, Green, 1928.

———, *Penal Legislation in the New Code of Canon Law*, revised by P. Lydon, New York: Benziger, 1936.

(Bachofen), Charles Augustine, *A Commentary on the New Code of Canon Law*, 8 vols., St. Louis: Herder, 1918-1922.

Barbosa, A., *Collectanea Doctorum in Varia Concilii Tridentini Decreta et Canones*, Lugduni, 1657.

Barrett, J., *A Comparative Study of the Councils of Baltimore and the Code of Canon Law*, The Catholic University of America Canon Law Studies, n. 83, Washington, D. C.: The Catholic University of America, 1932.

Benedictus XIV, *De Synodo Dioecesana*, 2 vols. in 1, Neapoli, 1772.

———, *Institutiones Ecclesiasticae* Romae, 1747.

Berutti, C., *Institutiones Iuris Canonici*, 6 vols., Vol. III, *De Religiosis*, Taurini-Romae: Marietti, 1936.

Beste, U., *Introductio in Codicem*, Collegeville, Minn.: St. John's Abbey Press, 1938.

Bevilacqua, A., *De Episcopi seu Ordinarii Iuribus ac Obligationibus*, Romae, 1921.

Biederlack, J.—Führich, M., *De Religiosis*, Oeniponte, 1919.

Blat, A., *Commentarium Textus Codicis Iuris Canonici*, 6 vols., Romae: Collegio "Angelico," 1921-1927.

Bolduc, G., *Les Études dans les Religions Cléricales*, The Catholic University of America Canon Law Studies, n. 149, Washington, D. C.: The Catholic University of America Press, 1942.

Bouix, D., *Tractatus de Episcopo*, ed. 2, 2 vols., Parisiis, 1873.

Bouuaert, F.—Simenon, G., *Manuale Juris Canonici*, Vols. I, III, ed. 3, 1930; Vol. II, 1931, Gandae et Leodii: Apud Auctores in Seminariis Gandavensi et Leodiensi.

Cappello, F., *Summa Iuris Canonici*, 3 vols., Romae: Apud Sedes Universitatis Gregorianae, 1930-1936.

———, *Tractatus Canonico-Moralis de Sacramentis*, 4 vols., Romae: Marietti, 1927-1932.

———, *Tractatus Canonico-Moralis de Censuris*, ed. altera, Taurinorum Augustae: Marietti, 1925.

Carbone, C., *Praxis Ordinandorum*, ed. altera, Taurini: Marietti, 1928.

Chelodi, J., *Ius de Personis iuxta Codicem Iuris Canonici*, ed. 2, ab E. Bertagnolli recognita et aucta, Tridenti: Libr. Edit. Tridentum, 1927.

———, *Ius Poenale et Ordo Procedendi in Iudiciis Criminalibus iuxta Codicem Iuris Canonici,* Tridenti: Libr. Edit. Tridentum, 1925 (1920?).

Chevalier, U., *Repertoire des Sources Historiques du Moyen Age* (topo-bibliographie), 2 vols., Montbeliard, 1894-1903.

Cicognani, H., *Canon Law,* ed. 2, Philadelphia: Dolphin Press, 1935.

Clancy, P., *The Local Religious Superior,* The Catholic University of America Canon Law Studies, n. 175, Washington, D. C.: The Catholic University of America Press, 1943.

Cocchi, G., *Commentarium in Codicem Iuris Canonici,* 8 vols., Lib. IV, *De Processibus,* Taurinorum Augustae; Marietti, 1930.

Coronata, M. Conte a, *Institutiones Iuris Canonici,* 5 vols., Taurini: Marietti, 1928-1936.

Cox, J., *The Administration of Seminaries,* The Catholic University of America Canon Law Studies, n. 67, Washington, D. C.: The Catholic University of America, 1931.

D'Annibale, J., *In Constitutionem Apostolicae Sedis Commentarii,* ed. 4, Prati, 1894.

De Angelis, P., *Praelectiones Iuris Canonici,* ed. N. Gentilini, 5 vols., Romae, 1908.

De Meester, A., *Juris Canonici et Juris Canonico-Civilis Compendium,* ed. nova, 3 vols. in 4, Brugis: Sumptibus et Typis Societatis Sancti Augustini, 1921-1928.

Devoti, J., *Institutionum Canonicarum Libri IV,* 4 vols., Romae, 1815.

Dictionnaire de Droit Canonique, Commencé sous la direction de A. Villien et E. Magnin; continué sous la direction de A. Amanieu et R. Naz, Fasc. 1-15, Paris—VI: Libraire Letouzey et Ane, 1924-1939.

Dubé, A., *The General Principles for the Reckoning of Time in Canon Law,* The Catholic University of America Canon Law Studies, n. 144, Washington, D. C.: The Catholic University of America Press, 1941.

Engel, L., *Collegium Universi Iuris Canonici,* ed. 10, Salisburgi, 1726.

Fabius Incarnatus, *Scrutinium Sacerdotale,* Venetiis, 1708.

Fagnanus, P., *Commentaria in Quinque Libros Decretalium,* 5 vols. in 3, Coloniae Allobrogum, 1759.

Fanfani, L., *De Iure Parochorum ad Normam Codicis Iuris Canonici,* Taurini-Romae: Marietti, 1924.

———, *De Iure Religiosorum ad Normam Codicis Iuris Canonici,* ed. 2, Taurini-Romae: Marietti, 1925.

Fermosini, N., *Opera Omnia Canonica, Civilia, et Criminalia,* ed. altera, 14 vols., Coloniae Allobrogum, 1741.

Ferraris, L., *Bibliotheca Canonica, Iuridico-Moralis Theologica partim Ascetica, Polemica, Rubricistica, Historica,* 8 vols., Bononiae, 1746.

Ferreres, J., *Compendium Theologiae Moralis,* ed. 15, 2 vols., Barcinone, 1932.

Gasparri, P., *Tractatus Canonicus de Sacra Ordinatione,* 2 vols., Parisiis, 1893-1894.

Giraldi, U., *Expositio Iuris Pontificii,* nova Romana ed., 2 vols., Romae, 1829-1830.

Gonzalez-Tellez, E., *Commentaria Perpetua in Singulos Textus Quinque Librorum Decretalium Gregorii IX,* 5 vols., Venetiis, 1699.

Guilfoyle, M., *Custom,* The Catholic University of America Canon Law Studies, n. 105, Washington, D. C.: The Catholic University of America, 1937.

Hallier, F., *De Sacris Electionibus et Ordinationibus ex Antiquo et Novo Ecclesiae Usu* (in Migne, J. P., *Theologiae Cursus Completus,* Vol. XXIV), Parisiis, 1860.

Hostiensis, Cardinalis (Henricus de Segusio), *Commentaria in Quinque Decretalium Libros,* 5 vols. in 3, Venetiis, 1581.

———, *Summa Aurea,* Venetiis, 1570.

Ioannes Andreae, *In VI Libros Decretalium Novella Commentaria,* 6 vols. in 5, Venetiis, 1570.

Jorio, D., *Sacerdos Alter Christus: De Instructione pro Scrutinio ad Ordines Peragendo Commentarius,* Romae: Sindacato Italiano Arti Grafiche, 1933.

Keene, M., *Religious Ordinaries and Canon 198,* The Catholic University of America Canon Law Studies, n. 135, Washington, D. C.: The Catholic University of America Press, 1942.

Lexicon für Theologie und Kirche, 10 vols., Freiburg im Breisgau: Herder, 1930-1938.

Louis, W., *Diocesan Archives,* The Catholic University of America Canon Law Studies, n. 137, Washington, D. C.: The Catholic University of America Press, 1941.

McBride, J., *Incardination and Excardination of Seculars,* The Catholic University of America Canon Law Studies, n. 145, Washington, D. C.: The Catholic University of America Press, 1941.

McCloskey, J., *The Subject of Ecclesiastical Law According to Canon 12,* The Catholic University of America Canon Law Studies, n. 165, Washington, D. C.: The Catholic University of America Press, 1943.

Many, S., *Praelectiones de Sacra Ordinatione,* Parisiis, 1905.

Marc, C.-Gestermann, F.-Raus, P., *Institutiones Morales Alphonsianae,* ed. 19, 2 vols., Lugduni: Typis Emmanuelis Vitte, 1933-1934.

Maroto, P., *Institutiones Iuris Canonici ad Normam Novi Codicis,* 2 vols., Tom. I, Matriti, 1919.

Moeder, J., *The Proper Bishop for Ordination and Dimissorial Letters,* The Catholic University of America Canon Law Studies, n. 95, Washington, D. C.: The Catholic University of America, 1935.

Monacelli, F., *Formularium Legale Practicum Fori Ecclesiastici,* 3 vols., Venetiis, 1736-1751.

Moriarity, E., *Oaths in Ecclesiastical Courts,* The Catholic University of America Canon Law Studies, n. 110, Washington, D. C.: The Catholic University of America, 1935.

Munerati, D., *Promptuarium pro Ordinandis et Confessariis Examinandis,* ed. 3, Romae, 1923.

Murphy, G., *Delinquencies and Penalties in the Administration and Reception of the Sacraments,* The Catholic University of America Canon Law Studies, n. 17, Washington, D. C.: The Catholic University of America, 1923.

Noval, I., *Commentarium Codicis Iuris Canonici,* Lib. IV, *De Processibus,* Pars I, *De Iudiciis,* Augustae Taurinorum-Romae, 1920.

O'Brien, J., *The Exemption of Religious in Church Law,* Milwaukee: Bruce, 1943.

O'Rourke, J., *Parish Registers,* The Catholic University of America Canon Law Studies, n. 88, Washington, D. C.: The Catholic University of America, 1934.

Ojetti, *Synopsis Rerum Moralium et Iuris Pontificii,* ed. 3, Romae, 1912.

Papi, H., *Religious in Church Law,* New York: Kenedy, 1924.

Passerini, P., *De Hominum Statibus et Officiis,* ed. emend., 3 vols., Lucae, 1732.

Pecorari, C., *Novum Manuale Ordinandorum,* 2 vols., Romae: Typis Polyglottis Vaticanis, 1929.

Pejska, I., *Ius Canonicum Religiosorum,* ed. 3, Friburgi Brisgoviae: Herder, 1927.

Pennachi, J., *Commentaria in Constitutionem Apostolicae Sedis,* 2 vols., Romae, 1883.

Petra, V., *Commentaria ad Constitutiones Apostolicas,* 5 vols., Venetiis, 1729.

Piatus Montensis, F., *Praelectiones Iuris Regularis,* ed. 3, 2 vols., Tornaci, 1906.

Prümmer, D., *Ius Regularium Speciale,* Friburgi Brisgoviae, 1907.

———, *Manuale Theologiae Moralis,* ed. 8, 3 vols., Friburgi Brisgoviae: Herder, 1935-1936.

Raus, P., *Institutiones Canonicae,* ed. altera, Lugduni-Parisiis: Typis Emmanuelis Vitte, 1931.

Raymundus de Pennafort, S., *Summa,* Veronae, 1744.

Reiffenstuel, A., *Jus Canonicum Universum,* 5 vols. in 7, Parisiis, 1864-1870.

Reilly, E., *The General Norms of Dispensation,* The Catholic University of America Canon Law Studies, n. 119, Washington, D. C.: The Catholic University of America Press, 1939.

Riganti, I., *Commentaria in Regulas, Constitutiones et Ordinationes Cancellariae Apostolicae,* 4 vols. in 2, Coloniae Allobrogum, 1751.

Roberts, J., *The Banns of Marriage,* The Catholic University of America Canon Law Studies, n. 64, Washington, D. C.: The Catholic University of America, 1931.

Roder, J., *Ordinandorum Enchiridion,* ed. altera curante M. Belli, Neapoli: Ex Typis Pontificiis M. D'Auria, 1928.

Rufinus, *Summa Decretorum,* ed. Singer, Paderborn, 1902.

Santi, F., *Praelectiones Iuris canonici,* ed. 4 cura Leitner, 5 vols. in 3, Ratisbonae, 1904-1905.

Schäfer, T., *De Religiosis ad Normam Codicis Iuris Canonici,* Münster: Aschendorff, 1927.

Schmalzgrueber, F., *Ius Eccelsiasticum Universum,* 5 vols. in 12, Romae, 1843-1845.

Sipos, S., *Enchiridion Iuris Canonici,* ed. altera, Pécs: Ex Typographia "Haladás R. T.," 1931.

Stadtmüller, R., *Das neue Ordensrecht,* Dülmen, 1919.

Swoboda, I., *Ignorance in Relation to the Imputability of Delicts,* The Catholic University of America Canon Law Studies, n. 143, Washington, D. C.: The Catholic University of America Press, 1941.

Téphany, J., *Constitution Apostolicae Sedis Commentaire,* Tours, 1883.

Thomas Aquinas, S., *Summa Theologica,* 5 vols., ed. 4 Faucher, Parisiis: Lethielleux, 1926.

Toso, A., *Ad Codicem Iuris Canonici Commentaria Minora,* 5 vols., Romae: Marietti, 1921-1927.

Vermeersch, A.-Creusen, J., *Epitome Iuris Canonici,* ed. 5, 3 vols., Mechliniae: Dessain, 1933-1936.

Vlaming, T., *Praelectiones Iuris Matrimonii,* ed. 3, 2 vols., Bussum, 1919-1921.

Waldron, J., *The Minister of Baptism,* The Catholic University of America Canon Law Studies, n. 170, Washington, D. C.: The Catholic University of America Press, 1942.

Wanenmacher, F., *Canonical Evidence in Marriage Cases,* Philadelphia: Dolphin Press, 1935.

Wernz, F. X., *Ius Decretalium,* 6 vols., Romae et Prati, 1898-1905.

Wernz, F. X.-Vidal, P., *Ius Canonicum,* 7 toms. in 9 vols., Romae: Apud Aedes Universitatis Gregorianae, 1923-1938.

Wigandt, M., *Tribunal Confessariorum et Ordinandorum,* ed. 3, Venetiis, 1717.

Willett, R., *The Probative Value of Documents in Ecclesiastical Trials,* The Catholic University of America Canon Law Studies, n. 171, Washington, D. C.: The Catholic University of America Press, 1942.

ARTICLES

Anonymous, "De studiis requisitis ante ordinationem"—*Periodica,* XII (1923), (9)-(10).

Goyeneche, S., "Consultationes"—*CpR,* III (1922), 263-4; VIII (1927), 376-9; *CpRM,* XIX (1938), 14-8; 84-7.

Hannan, J., "Ordinations at Christmas"—*The Jurist,* I (1941), 153-4.

———, "Ex-Seminarian and Novice"—*The Jurist,* II (1942), 380-2.

Larraona, A., "Animadversiones"—*Apollinaris,* IV (1931), 207-8.

———, "Commentarium Codicis"—*CpR,* IV (1923), 39-46; XIX (1938), 154-60.

———, "Consultationes"—*CpR,* V (1924), 102-4.

———, "Quaestio Canonica"—*CpR,* IV (1923), 113-9.

Lopez, U., "De inquisitione circa pietatem ordinandorum et de animi libertate in usu Communionis frequentis"—*Periodica,* XXIX (1940), 302-7.

Maroto, P., "Annotationes"—*CpR,* II (1921), 98-101; XIII (1932), 175-80.

Oesterle, G., "De ratione studiorum in religionibus clericalibus"—*CpR,* VI (1925), 296-323.

Saucedo, P., "Exercitium Jurisdictionis et Superiores Laici ex Ordine Hospitalario S. Joannis de Deo"—*CpR,* XIII (1932), 51-61; 106-14; 224-31; 291-302.

Schaaf, V., "Episcopus Proprius Ordinationis Religiosorum"—*AER,* XC (1934), 491-509.

Schmidt, J., "Juridic Value of the *Instructio*"—*The Jurist,* I (1941), 289-316.

Vermeersch, A., "Annotationes"—*Periodica,* XXI (1932), 188-93.

———, "Partes Confessarii in diudicanda virtute necessaria ad sacros ordines" —*Periodica,* XVII (1928), 231*-41*.

Voltas, P., "De domicilio quoad ordinationem religiosorum"—*CpR,* II (1921), 299-307.

Vromant, G., "De signis negativis vocationis sacerdotalis et religiosae"—*Periodica,* XXII (1933), 187*-91*.

PERIODICALS

American Ecclesiastical Review, The (formerly *The Ecclesiastical Review),* Philadelphia, 1889-1943; Baltimore, 1944—

Ami du Clergé, L', Paris, Langres, 1878—

Apollinaris, Romae, 1928—

Archiv für katholisches Kirchenrecht, Innsbruck, 1857-1861; Mainz, 1862—

Commentarium pro Religiosis, Romae, 1920—; ab anno 1935: *Commentarium pro Religiosis et Missionariis.*

Homiletic and Pastoral Review, The, New York, 1900—

Jurist, The, Washiington, D. C., 1941—

Periodica de Re Canonica et Morali Utili praesertim Religiosis et Missionariis, Brugis, 1905— ; ab anno 1927: *Periodica de Re Canonica, Morali, Liturgica.*

ABBREVIATIONS

AAS—Acta Apostolicae Sedis.
AER—The American Ecclesiastical Review.
AKKR—Archiv für katholisches Kirchenrecht.
ASS—Acta Sanctae Sedis.
c.—canon seu caput (iuris antiqui).
cc.—canones seu capita (iuris antiqui).
can.—canon (novi Codicis).
cans.—canones (novi Codicis).
Coll. Lac.—Acta et Decreta Sacrorum Conciliorum Recentiorum, Collectio Lacensis.
CpR(M)—Commentarium pro Religiosis (et Missionariis).
Fontes—Codicis Iuris Canonici Fontes.
Mansi—Sacrorum Conciliorum Nova et Amplissima Collectio.
MGH—Monumenta Germaniae Historica.
MPG—Migne, Patrologia Graeca.
MPL—Migne, Patrologia Latina.
Periodica—Periodica de Re Canonica, Morali, Liturgica.
PCI—Pontifical Commission for the Authentic Interpretation of the Canons of the Code.
Quam ingens—S.C. de Sacr., instr., 27 dec. 1930.
Quantum Religiones—S.C. de Rel., instr., 1 dec. 1931.
S.C.C.—Sacra Congregatio Concilii.
S.C. de Prop. Fide—Sacra Congregatio de Propaganda Fide.
S.C. de Rel.—Sacra Congregatio de Religiosis.
S.C. de Sacr.—Sacra Congregatio de Sacramentis.
S.C. de Sem. et Stud. Univ.—Sacra Congregatio de Seminariis et Studiorum Universitatibus.
S.C.Ep. et Reg.—Sacra Congregatio Episcoporum et Regularium.
S.C. pro Eccl. Orient.—Sacra Congregatio pro Ecclesia Orientali.
S.C.S. Off.—Sacra Congregatio Sancti Offici.
Thesaurus—Thesaurus Resolutionum Sacrae Congregationis Concilii.

BIOGRAPHICAL NOTE

Thomas Raphael Gallagher was born on June 14, 1914, in New York City and received his early education at Annunciation Parochial School and Regis High School of that city. After completing two years at Providence College, he entered the novitiate of the Order of Preachers at Springfield, Kentucky, in August, 1933. In the following year he made simple profession and was sent to the Dominican House of Studies, River Forest, Illinois, for his philosophical studies. He was granted the Bachelor of Arts degree in June, 1937, and was solemnly professed on August 16th of the same year. After the first year of theology he continued his studies at the Dominican House of Studies, Washington, D. C. He was ordained to the priesthood on May 31, 1940. On the completion of the fourth year of theology, he received the degree of Lector of Sacred Theology. In September, 1941, he entered the School of Canon Law at the Catholic University of America and was granted the degree of the Baccalaureate in Canon Law in May, 1942, and the degree of the Licentiate in Canon Law in May, 1943.

ALPHABETICAL INDEX

CANON LAW STUDIES*

1. Freriks, Rev. Celestine A., C.PP.S., J.C.D., Religious Congregations in Their External Relations, 121 pp., 1916.
2. Galliher, Rev. Daniel M., O.P., J.C.D., Canonical Elections, 117 pp. 1917.
3. Borkowski, Rev. Aurelius L., O.F.M., J.C.D., De Confraternitatibus Ecclesiasticis, 136 pp., 1918.
4. Castillo, Rev. Cayo, J.C.D., Disertacion Historico-Canonica sobre la Potestad del Cabildo en Sede Vacante o Impedida del Vicario Capitular, 99 pp., 1919 (1918).
5. Kubelbeck, Rev. William J., S.T.B., J.C.D., The Sacred Penitentiaria and Its Relation to Faculties of Ordinaries and Priests, 129 pp., 1918.
6. Petrovits, Rev. Joseph, J.C., S.T.D., J.C.D., The New Church Law on Matrimony, X-461 pp., 1919.
7. Hickey, Rev. John J., S.T.B., J.C.D., Irregularities and Simple Impediments in the New Code of Canon Law, 100 pp., 1920.
8. Klekotka, Rev. Peter J., S.T.B., J.C.D., Diocesan Consultors, 179 pp., 1920.
9. Wanenmacher, Rev. Francis, J.C.D., The Evidence in Ecclesiastical Procedure Affecting the Marriage Bond, 1920 (Printed 1935).
10. Golden, Rev. Henry Francis, J.C.D., Parochial Benefices in the New Code, IV-119 pp., 1921 (Printed 1925).
11. Koudelka, Rev. Charles J., J.C.D., Pastors, Their Rights and Duties According to the New Code of Canon Law, 211 pp., 1921.
12. Melo, Rev. Antonius, O.F.M., J.C.D., De Exemptione Regularium, X-188 pp., 1921.
13. Schaaf, Rev. Valentine Theodore, O.F.M., S.T.B., J.C.D., The Cloister, X-180 pp., 1921.
14. Burke, Rev. Thomas Joseph, S.T.D., J.C.D., Competence in Ecclesiastical Tribunals, IV-117 pp., 1922.
15. Leech, Rev. George Leo, J.C.D., A Comparative Study of the Constitution "Apostolicae Sedis" and the "Codex Juris Canonici," 179 pp., 1922.
16. Motry, Rev. Hubert Louis, S.T.D., J.C.D., Diocesan Faculties According to the Code of Canon Law, II-167 pp., 1922.
17. Murphy, Rev. George Lawrence, J.C.D., Delinquencies and Penalties in the Administration and the Reception of the Sacraments, IV-121 pp., 1923.
18. O'Reilly, Rev. John Anthony, S.T.B., J.C.D., Ecclesiastical Sepulture in the New Code of Canon Law, II-129 pp., 1923.

* Below n. 100 only the following numbers are still available: Nn. 3, 4, 9, 25, 34, 57 and 75. Beginning with n. 100 only the following are unavailable: Nn. 100-111, and n. 113.

19. Michalicka, Rev. Wenceslas Cyrill, O.S.B., J.C.D., Judicial Procedure in Dismissal of Clerical Exempt Religious, 107 pp., 1923.
20. Dargin, Rev. Edward Vincent, S.T.B., J.C.D., Reserved Cases According to the Code of Canon Law, IV-103 pp., 1924.
21. Godfrey, Rev. John A., S.T.B., J.C.D., The Right of Patronage According to the Code of Canon Law, 153 pp., 1924.
22. Hagedorn, Rev. Francis Edward, J.C.D., General Legislation on Indulgences, II-154 pp., 1924.
23. King, Rev. James Ignatius, J.C.D., The Administration of the Sacraments to Dying Non-Catholics, V-141 pp., 1924.
24. Winslow, Rev. Francis Joseph, O.F.M., J.C.D., Vicars and Prefects Apostolic, IV-149 pp., 1924.
25. Correa, Rev. Jose Servelion, S.T.L., J.C.D., La Potestad Legislativa de la Iglesia Catholica, IV-127 pp., 1925.
26. Dugan, Rev. Henry Francis, A.M., J.C.D., The Judiciary Department of the Diocesan Curia, 87 pp., 1925.
27. Keller, Rev. Charles Frederick, S.T.B., J.C.D., Mass Stipends, 167 pp., 1925.
28. Paschang, Rev. John Linus, J.C.D., The Sacramentals According to the Code of Canon Law, 129 pp., 1925.
29. Piontek, Rev. Cyrillus, O.F.M., S.T.B., J.C.D., De Indulto Exclaustrationis necnon Saecularizationis, XIII-289 pp., 1925.
30. Kearney, Rev. Richard Joseph, S.T.B., J.C.D., Sponsors at Baptism According to the Code of Canon Law, IV-127 pp., 1925.
31. Bartlett, Rev. Chester Joseph, A.M., LL.B., J.C.D., The Tenure of Parochial Property in the United States of America, V-108 pp., 1926.
32. Kilker, Rev. Adrian Jerome, J.C.D., Extreme Unction, V-425 pp., 1926.
33. McCormick, Rev. Robert Emmett, J.C.D., Confessors of Religious, VIII-266 pp., 1926.
34. Miller, Rev. Newton Thomas, J.C.D., Founded Masses According to the Code of Canon Law, VII-93 pp., 1926.
35. Roelker, Rev. Edward G., S.T.D., J.C.D., Principles of Privilege According to the Code of Canon Law, XI-166 pp., 1926.
36. Bakalarczyk, Rev. Richardus, M.I.C., J.U.D., De Novitiatu, VIII-208 pp., 1927.
37. Pizzuti, Rev. Lawrence, O.F.M., J.U.L., De Parochis Religiosis, 1927. (Not Printed.)
38. Bliley, Rev. Nicholas Martin, O.S.B., J.C.D., Altars According to the Code of Canon Law, XIX-132 pp., 1927.
39. Brown, Mr. Brendan Francis, A.B., LL.M., J.U.D., The Canonical Juristic Personality with Special Reference to its Status in the United States of America, V-212 pp., 1927.
40. Cavanaugh, Rev. William Thomas, C.P., J.U.D., The Reservation of the Blessed Sacrament, VIII-101 pp., 1927.

41. DOHENY, REV. WILLIAM J., C.S.C., A.B., J.U.D., Church Property: Modes of Acquisition, X-118 pp., 1927.
42. FELDHAUS, REV. ALOYSIUS H., C.PP.S., J.C.D., Oratories, IX-141 pp., 1927.
43. KELLY, REV. JAMES PATRICK, A.B., J.C.D., The Jurisdiction of the Simple Confessor, X-208 pp., 1927.
44. NEUBERGER, REV. NICHOLAS J., J.C.D., Canon 6 or the Relation of the Codex Juris Canonici to the Preceding Legislation, V-95 pp., 1927.
45. O'KEEFE, REV. GERALD MICHAEL, J.C.D., Matrimonial Dispensations, Powers of Bishops, Priests, and Confessors, VIII-232 pp., 1927.
46. QUIGLEY, REV. JOSEPH A. M., A.B., J.C.D., Condemned Societies, 139 pp., 1927.
47. ZAPLOTNIK, REV. JOHANNES LEO, J.C.D., De Vicariis Foraneis, X-142 pp., 1927.
48. DUSKIE, REV. JOHN ALOYSIUS, A.B., J.C.D., The Canonical Status of the Orientals in the United States, VIII-196 pp., 1928.
49. HYLAND, REV. FRANCIS EDWARD, J.C.D., Excommunication, Its Nature, Historical Development and Effects, VIII-181 pp., 1928.
50. REINMANN, REV. GERALD JOSEPH, O.M.C., J.C.D., The Third Order Secular of Saint Francis, 201 pp., 1928.
51. SCHENK, REV. FRANCIS J., J.C.D., The Matrimonial Impediments of Mixed Religion and Disparity of Cult, XVI-318 pp., 1929.
52. COADY, REV. JOHN JOSEPH, S.T.D., J.U.D., A.M., The Appointment of Pastors, VIII-150 pp., 1929.
53. KAY, REV. THOMAS HENRY, J.C.D., Competence in Matrimonial Procedure, VIII-164 pp., 1929.
54. TURNER, REV. SIDNEY JOSEPH, C.P., J.U.D., The Vow of Poverty, XLIX-217 pp., 1929.
55. KEARNEY, REV. RAYMOND A., A.B., S.T.D., J.C.D., The Principles of Delegation, VII-149 pp., 1929.
56. CONRAN, REV. EDWARD JAMES, A.B., J.C.D., The Interdict, V-163 pp., 1930.
57. O'NEILL, REV. WILLIAM H., J.C.D., Papal Rescripts of Favor, VII-218 pp., 1930.
58. BASTNAGEL, REV. CLEMENT VINCENT, J.U.D., The Appointment of Parochial Adjutants and Assistants, XV-257 pp., 1930.
59. FERRY, REV. WILLIAM A., A.B., J.C.D., Stole Fees, V-136 pp., 1930.
60. COSTELLO, REV. JOHN MICHAEL, A.B., J.C.D., Domicile and Quasi-Domicile, VII-201 pp., 1930.
61. KREMER, REV. MICHAEL NICHOLAS, A.B., S.T.D., J.C.D., Church Support in the United States, VI-136 pp., 1930.
62. ANGULO, REV. LUIS, C.M., J.C.D., Legislation de la Iglesia sobre la intencion en la application de la Santa Misa, VII-104 pp., 1931.
63. FREY, REV. WOLFGANG NORBERT, O.S.B., A.B., J.C.D., The Act of Religious Profession, VII-174 pp., 1931.
64. ROBERTS, REV. JAMES BRENDAN, A.B., J.C.D., The Banns of Marriage, XIV-140 pp., 1931.

65. RYDER, REV. RAYMOND ALOYSIUS, A.B., J.C.D., Simony, IX-151 pp., 1931.
66. CAMPAGNA, REV. ANGELO, PH.D., J.U.D., Il Vicario Generale del Vescovo, VII-205 pp., 1931.
67. COX, REV. JOSEPH GODFREY, A.B., J.C.D., The Administration of Seminaries, VI-124 pp., 1931.
68. GREGORY, REV. DONALD J., J.U.D., The Pauline Privilege, XV-165 pp., 1931.
69. DONOHUE, REV. JOHN F., J.C.D., The Impediment of Crime, VII-110 pp., 1931.
70. DOOLEY, REV. EUGENE A., O.M.I., J.C.D., Church Law on Sacred Relics, IX-143 pp., 1931.
71. ORTH, REV. CLEMENT RAYMOND, O.M.C., J.C.D., The Approbation of Religious Institutes, 171 pp., 1931.
72. PERNICONE, REV. JOSEPH M., A.B., J.C.D., The Ecclesiastical Prohibition of Books, XII-267 pp., 1932.
73. CLINTON, REV. CONNELL, A.B., J.C.D., The Paschal Precept, IX-108 pp., 1932.
74. DONNELLY, REV. FRANCIS B., A.M., S.T.L., J.C.D., The Diocesan Synod, VIII-125 pp., 1932.
75. TORRENTE, REV. CAMILO, C.M.F., J.C.D., Las Processiones Sagradas, V-145 pp., 1932.
76. MURPHY, REV. EDWIN J., C.PP.S., J.C.D., Suspension Ex Informata Conscientia, XI-122 pp., 1932.
77. MACKENZIE, REV. ERIC F., A.M., S.T.L., J.C.D., The Delict of Heresy in Its Commission, Penalization, Absolution, VII-124 pp., 1932.
78. LYONS, REV. AVITUS E., S.T.B., J.C.D., The Collegiate Tribunal of First Instance, XI-147 pp., 1932.
79. CONNOLLY, REV. THOMAS A., J.C.D., Appeals, XI-195 pp., 1932.
80. SANGMEISTER, REV. JOSEPH V., A.B., J.C.D., Force and Fear as Precluding Matrimonial Consent, V-211 pp., 1932.
81. JAEGER, REV. LEO A., A.B., J.C.D., The Administration of Vacant and Quasi-Vacant Episcopal Sees in the United States, IX-229 pp., 1932.
82. RIMLINGER, REV. HERBERT T., J.C.D., Error Invalidating Matrimonial Consent, VII-79 pp., 1932.
83. BARRETT, REV. JOHN D. M., S.S., J.C.D., A Comparative Study of the Third Plenary Council of Baltimore and the Code, IX-221 pp., 1932.
84. CARBERRY, REV. JOHN J., PH.D., S.T.D., J.C.D., The Juridical Form of Marriage, X-177 pp., 1934.
85. DOLAN, REV. JOHN L., A.B., J.C.D., The Defensor Vinculi, XII-157 pp., 1934
86. HANNAN, REV. JEROME D., A.M., S.T.D., LL.B., J.C.D., The Canon Law of Wills, IX-517 pp., 1934.
87. LEMIEUX, REV. DELISE A., A.M., J.C.D., The Sentence in Ecclesiastical Procedure, IX-131 pp., 1934.
88. O'ROURKE, REV. JAMES J., A.B., J.C.D., Parish Registers, VII-109 pp., 1934.

89. Timlin, Rev. Bartholomew, O.F.M., A.M., J.C.D., Conditional Matrimonial Consent, X-381 pp., 1934.
90. Wahl, Rev. Francis X., A.B., J.C.D., The Matrimonial Impediments of Consanguinity and Affinity, VI-125 pp., 1934.
91. White, Rev. Robert J., A.B., LL.B., S.T.B., J.C.D., Canonical Ante-Nuptial Promises and the Civil Law, VI-152 pp., 1934.
92. Herrera, Rev. Antonio Parra, O.C.D., J.C.D., Legislation Ecclesiastica sobra el Ayuno y la Abstinencia, XI-191 pp., 1935.
93. Kennedy, Rev. Edwin J., J.C.D., The Special Matrimonial Process in Cases of Evident Nullity, X-165 pp., 1935.
94. Manning, Rev. John J., A.B., J.C.D., Presumption of Law in Matrimonial Procedure, XI-111 pp., 1935.
95. Moeder, Rev. John M., J.C.D., The Proper Bishop for Ordination and Dimissorial Letters, VII-135 pp., 1935.
96. O'Mara, Rev. William A., A.B., J.C.D., Canonical Causes for Matrimonial Dispensations, IX-155 pp., 1935.
97. Reilly, Rev. Peter, J.C.D., Residence of Pastors, IX-81 pp., 1935.
98. Smith, Rev. Mariner T., O.P., S.T.Lr., J.C.D., The Penal Law for Religious, VII-169 pp., 1935.
99. Whalen, Rev. Donald W., A.M., J.C.D., The Value of Testimonial Evidence in Matrimonial Procedure, XIII-297 pp., 1935.
100. Cleary, Rev. Joseph F., J.C.D., Canonical Limitations on the Alienation of Church Property, VIII-141 pp., 1936.
101. Glynn, Rev. John C., J.C.D., The Promoter of Justice, XX-337 pp., 1936.
102. Brennan, Rev. James H., SS., M.A., S.T.B., J.C.D., The Simple Convalidation of Marriage, VI-135 pp., 1937.
103. Brunini, Rev. Joseph Bernard, J.C.D., The Clerical Obligations of Canons 139 and 142, X-121 pp., 1937.
104. Connor, Rev. Maurice, A.B., J.C.D., The Administrative Removal of Pastors, VIII-159 pp., 1937.
105. Guilfoyle, Rev. Merlin Joseph, J.C.D., Custom, XI-144 pp., 1937.
106. Hughes, Rev. James Austin, A.B., A.M., J.C.D., Witnesses in Criminal Trials of Clerics, IX-140 pp., 1937.
107. Jansen, Rev. Raymond J., A.B., S.T.L., J.C.D., Canonical Provisions for Catechetical Instruction, VII-153 pp., 1937.
108. Kealy, Rev. John James, A.B., J.C.D., The Introductory Libellus in Church Court Procedure, XI-121 pp., 1937.
109. McManus, Rev. James Edward, C.SS.R., J.C.D., The Administration of Temporal Goods in Religious Institutes, XVI-196 pp., 1937.
110. Moriarty, Rev. Eugene James, J.C.D., Oaths in Ecclesiastical Courts, X-115 pp., 1937.
111. Rainer, Rev. Eligius George, C.SS.R., J.C.D., Suspension of Clerics, XVII-249 pp., 1937.
112. Reilly, Rev. Thomas F., C.SS.R., J.C.D., Visitation of Religious, VI-195 pp., 1938.

113. MORIARTY, REV. FRANCIS E., C.SS.R., J.C.D., The Extraordinary Absolution from Censures, XV-334 pp., 1938.
114. CONNOLLY, REV. NICHOLAS P., J.C.D., The Canonical Erection of Parishes, X-132 pp., 1938.
115. DONOVAN, REV. JAMES JOSEPH, J.C.D., The Pastor's Obligation in Prenuptial Investigation, XII-322 pp., 1938.
116. HARRIGAN, REV. ROBERT J., M.A., S.T.B., J.C.D., The Radical Sanation of Invalid Marriages, VIII-208 pp., 1938.
117. BOFFA, REV. CONRAD HUMBERT, J.C.D., Canonical Provisions for Catholic Schools, VII-211 pp., 1939.
118. PARSONS, REV. ANSCAR JOHN, O.M.Cap., J.C.D., Canonical Elections, XII-236 pp., 1939.
119. REILLY, REV. EDWARD MICHAEL, A.B., J.C.D., The General Norms of Dispensation, XII-156 pp., 1939.
120. RYAN, REV. GERALD ALOYSIUS, A.B., J.C.D., Principles of Episcopal Jurisdiction, XII-172 pp., 1939.
121. BURTON, REV. FRANCIS JAMES, C.S.C., A.B., J.C.D., A Commentary on Canon 1125, X-222 pp., 1940.
122. MIASKIEWICZ, REV. FRANCIS SIGISMUND, J.C.D., Supplied Jurisdiction According to Canon 209, XII-340 pp., 1940.
123. RICE, REV. PATRICK WILLIAM, A.B., J.C.D., Proof of Death in Prenuptial Investigation, VIII-156 pp., 1940.
124. ANGLIN, REV. THOMAS FRANCIS, M.S., J.C.D., The Eucharistic Fast, VIII-183 pp., 1941.
125. COLEMAN, REV. JOHN JEROME, J.C.D., The Minister of Confirmation, VI-153 pp., 1941.
126. DOWNS, REV. JOSEPH EMMANUEL, A.B., J.C.D., The Concept of Clerical Immunity, XI-163 pp., 1941.
127. ESSWEIN, REV. ANTHONY ALBERT, J.C.D., Extrajudicial Penal Powers of Ecclesiastical Superiors, X-144 pp., 1941.
128. FARRELL, REV. BENJAMIN FRANCIS, M.A., S.T.L., J.C.D., The Rights and Duties of the Local Ordinary Regarding Congregations of Women Religious of Pontifical Appıoval, V-195 pp., 1941.
129. FEENEY, REV. THOMAS JOHN, A.B., S.T.L., J.C.D., Restitutio in Integrum, VI-169 pp., 1941.
130. FINDLAY, REV. STEPHEN WILLIAM, O.S.B., A.B., J.C.D., Canonical Norms Governing the Deposition and Degradation of Clerics, XVII-279 pp., 1941.
131. GOODWINE, REV. JOHN, A.B., S.T.L., J.C.D., The Right of the Church to Acquire Property, VIII-119 pp., 1941.
132. HESTON, REV. EDWARD LOUIS, C.S.C., PH.D., S.T.D., J.C.D., The Alienation of Church Property in the United States, XII-222 pp., 1941.
133. HOGAN, REV. JAMES JOHN, A.B., S.T.L., J.C.D., Judicial Advocates and Procurators, XIII-200 pp., 1941.

134. KEALTY, REV. THOMAS M., A.B., LITT.B., J.C.D., Dowry of Women Religious, IX-152 pp., 1941.
135. KEENE, REV. MICHAEL JAMES, O.S.B., J.C.D., Religious Ordinaries and Canon 198, V-164 pp., 1942.
136. KERIN, REV. CHARLES A., S.S., M.A., S.T.B., J.C.D., The Privation of Christian Burial, XVI-279 pp., 1941.
137. LOUIS, REV. WILLIAM FRANCIS, M.A., J.C.D., Diocesan Archives, X-101 pp., 1941.
138. MCDEVITT, REV. GILBERT JOSEPH, A.B., J.C.D., Legitimacy and Legitimation, X-247 pp., 1941.
139. MCDONOUGH, REV. THOMAS JOSEPH, A.B., J.C.D., Apostolic Administration, X-217 pp., 1941.
140. MEIER, REV. CARL ANTHONY, A.B., J.C.D., Penal Administrative Procedure Against Negligent Pastors, XI-240 pp., 1941.
141. SCHMIDT, REV. JOHN ROGG, A.B., J.C.D., The Principles of Authentic Interpretation in Canon 17 of the Code of Canon Law, XII-331 pp., 1941.
142. SLAFKOSKY, REV. ANDREW LEONARD, A.B., J.C.D., The Canonical Episcopal Visitation of the Diocese, X-197 pp., 1941.
143. SWOBODA, REV. INNOCENT ROBERT, O.F.M., J.C.D., Ignorance in Relation to the Imputability of Delicts, IX-271 pp., 1941.
144. DUBE, REV. ARTHUR JOSEPH, A.B., J.C.D., The General Principles for the Reckoning of Time in Canon Law, VIII-299 pp., 1941.
145. MCBRIDE, REV. JAMES T., A.B., J.C.D., Incardination and Excardination of Seculars, XX-585 pp., 1941.
146. KROL, REV. JOHN T., J.C.D., The Defendant in Ecclesiastical Trials, XII-207 pp., 1942.
147. COMYNS, REV. JOSEPH J., C.SS.R., A.B., J.C.D., Papal and Episcopal Administration of Church Property, XIV-155 pp., 1942.
148. BARRY, REV. GARRETT FRANCIS, O.M.I., J.C.D., Violation of the Cloister, XII-260 pp., 1942.
149. BOLDUC, REV. GATIEN, C.S.V., A.B., S.T.L., J.C.D., Les Études dans les Religious Cléricales, VIII-155 pp., 1942.
150. BOYLE, REV. DAVID JOHN, M.A., J.C.D., The Juridic Effects of Moral Certitude on Pre-Nuptial Guarantees, XII-188 pp., 1942.
151. CANAVAN, REV. WALTER JOSEPH, M.A., LITT.D., J.C.D., The Profession of Faith, XII-143 pp., 1942.
152. DESROCHERS, REV. BRUNO, A.B., PH.D., S.T.B., J.C.D., Le Premier Concile Plénier de Québec et le Code de Droit Canonique, XIV-186 pp., 1942.
153. DILLON, REV. ROBERT EDWARD, A.B., J.C.D., Common Law Marriage, X-148 pp., 1942.
154. DODWELL, REV. EDWARD JOHN, PH.D., S.T.B., J.C.D., The Time and Place for the Celebration of Marriage, X-156 pp., 1942.
155. DONNELLAN, REV. THOMAS ANDREW, A.B., J.C.D., The Obligation of the Missa pro Populo, VII-131 pp., 1942.
156. ELTZ, REV. LOUIS ANTHONY, A.B., J.C.L., Cooperation in Crime.

157. GASS, REV. SYLVESTER FRANCIS, M.A., J.C.D., Ecclesiastical Pensions, XI-206 pp., 1942.
158. GUINIVEN, REV. JOHN JOSEPH, C.SS.R., J.C.D., The Precept of Hearing Mass-188 pp., 1942.
159. GULCZYNSKI, REV. JOHN THEOPHILUS, J.C.D., The Desecration and Violation of Churches, X-126 pp., 1942.
160. HAMMILL, REV. JOHN LEO, M.A., J.C.D., The Obligations of the Traveler According to Canon 14, VIII-204 pp., 1942.
161. HAYDT, REV. JOHN JOSEPH, A.B., J.C.D., Reserved Benefices, XI-148 pp., 1942.
162. HUSER, REV. ROGER JOHN, O.F.M., A.B., J.C.D., The Crime of Abortion in Canon Law, XII-187 pp., 1942.
163. KEARNEY, REV. FRANCIS PATRICK, A.B., S.T.L.,. J.C.L., The Principles of Canon 1127.
164. LINAHEN, REV. LEO JAMES, S.T.L., J.C.D., De Absolutione Complicis in Peccato Turpi, 114 pp., 1942.
165. MCCLOSKEY, REV. JOSEPH ALOYSIUS, A.B., J.C.D., The Subject of Ecclesiastical Law According to Canon 12, XVII-246 pp., 1942.
166. O'NEILL, REV. FRANCIS JOSEPH, C.SS.R., J.C.D., The Dismissal of Religious in Temporary Vows, XIII-220 pp., 1942.
167. PRINCE, REV. JOHN EDWARD, A.B., S.T.B., J.C.D., The Diocesan Chancellor, X-136 pp., 1942.
168. RIESNER, REV. ALBERT JOSEPH, C.SS.R., J.C.D., Apostates and Fugitives from Religious Institutes, IX-168 pp., 1942.
169. STENGER, REV. JOSEPH BERNARD, J.C.D., The Mortgaging of Church Property, 186 pp., 1942.
170. WALDRON, REV. JOSEPH FRANCIS, A.B., J.C.D., The Minister of Baptism, XII-197 pp., 1942.
171. WILLETT, REV. ROBERT ALBERT, J.C.D., The Probative Value of Documents In Ecclesiastical Trials, X-124 pp., 1942.
172.. WOEBER, REV. EDWARD MARTIN, M.A., J.C.D., The Interpellations, XII-pp., 1942
173. BENKO, REV. MATTHEW ALOYSIUS, O.S.B., M.A., J.C.L., The Abbot *Nullius*.
174. CHRIST, REV. JOSEPH JAMES, M.A., S.T.L., J.C.L., Dispensation from Vindicative Penalties.
175. CLANCY, REV. PATRICK M. J., O.P., A.B., S.T.LR., J.C.D., The Local Religious Superior, X-229 pp., 1943.
176. CLARKE, REV. THOMAS JAMES, J.C.D., Parish Societies, XII-147 pp., 1943.
177. CONNOLLY, REV. JOHN PATRICK, S.T.L., J.C.D., Synodal Examiners and Parish Priest Consultors, X-223 pp., 1943.
178. DRUMM, REV. WILLIAM MARTIN, A.B., J.C.L., Hospital Chaplains.
179. FLANAGAN, REV. BERNARD JOSEPH, A.B., S.T.L., J.C.D., The Canonical Erection of Religious Houses, X-147 pp., 1943.
180. KELLEHER, REV. STEPHEN JOSEPH, A.B., S.T.B., J.C.D., Discussions with non-Catholics: Canonical Legislation, X-93 pp., 1943.

181. LEWIS, REV. GORDIAN, C.P., J.C.D., Chapters in Religious Institutes, XII-169 pp., 1943.
182. MARX, REV. ADOLPH, J.C.D., The Declaration of Nullity of Marriages Contracted Outside the Church, X-151 pp., 1943.
183. MATULENAS, REV. RAYMOND ANTHONY, O.S.B., A.B., J.C.L., Communication, a Source of Privileges.
184. O'LEARY, REV. CHARLES GERARD, C.SS.R., J.C.L., Religious Dismissed After Perpetual Profession.
185. POWER, REV. CORNELIUS MICHAEL, J.C.L., The Blessing of Cemeteries.
186. SHUHLER, REV. RALPH VINCENT, O.S.A., J.C.D., Privileges of Regulars to Absolve and Dispense, XII-195 pp., 1943.
187. ZIOLKOWSKI, REV. THADDEUS STANISLAUS, A.B., J.C.D., The Consecration and Blessing of Churches, XII-151 pp., 1943.
188. HENEGHAN, REV. JOHN JOSEPH, S.T.D., J.C.L., The Marriages of Unworthy Catholics: Canons 1065 and 1066.
189. CARROLL, REV. COLEMAN FRANCIS, M.A., S.T.L., J.C.L., Charitable Institutions.
190. CIESLUK, REV. JOSEPH EDWARD, PH.B., S.T.L., J.C.L., National Parishes in the United States.
191. COBURN, REV. VINCENT PAUL, A.B., J.C.L., Marriages of Conscience.
192. CONNORS, REV. CHARLES PAUL, C.S.SP., A.B., J.C.L., Extra-Judicial Procurators in the Code of Canon Law.
193. COYLE, REV. PAUL RAYMOND, A.B., J.C.L., Judicial Exceptions.
194. FAIR, REV. BARTHOLOMEW FRANCIS, A.B., S.T.L., J.C.L., The Impediment of Abduction.
195. GALLAGHER, REV. THOMAS RAPHAEL, O.P., A.B., S.T.LR., J.C.L., The Examination of the Qualities of the Ordinand.
196. GANNON, REV. JOHN MARK, S.T.L., J.C.L., The Interstices Required for the Promotion to Orders.
197. GOLDSMITH, REV. J. WILLIAM, B.C.S., S.T.L., J.C.L., The Competence of Church and State over Marriage—Disputed Points.
198. GOODWINE, REV. JOSEPH GERARD, A.B., S.T.B., J.C.L., The Reception of Converts.
199. KOWALSKI, REV. ROMUALD EUGENE, O.F.M., A.B., J.C.L., Sustenance of Religious Houses of Regulars.
200. MCCOY, REV. ALAN EDWARD, O.F.M., Force and Fear in Relation to Delictual Imputability and Penal Responsibility.
201. MCDEVITT, REV. VINCENT JOHN, PH.B., S.T.L., J.C.L., Perjury.
202. MARTIN, REV. THOMAS OWEN, PH.D., S.T.D., J.C.L., Adverse Possession, Prescription and Limitation of Actions: The Canonical "Praescriptio."
203. MIKLOSOVIC, REV. PAUL JOHN, A.B., J.C.L., Attempted Marriages and Their Consequent Juridic Effects.
204. MUNDY, REV. THOMAS MAURICE, A.B., S.T.L., J.C.L., The Union of Parishes.

205. O'DEA, REV. JOHN COYLE, A.B., J.C.L., The Matrimonial Impediment of Nonage.
206. OLALIA, REV. ALEXANDER AYSON, S.T.L., J.C.L., A Comparative Study of the Christian Constitution of States and the Constitution of the Philippine Commonwealth.
207. POISSON, REV. PIERRE-MARIE, C.S.C., A.B., PH.L., TH.L., J.C.L., Droits Patrimoniaux des Maisons ed des Eglises Religieuses.
208. STADALNIKAS, REV. CASIMIR JOSEPH, M.I.C., J.C.L., Reservation of Censures.
209. SULLIVAN, REV. EUGENE HENRY, S.T.L., J.C.L., Proof of the Reception of the Sacraments.
210. VAUGHAN, REV. WILLIAM EDWARD, J.C.L., Constitutions for Diocesan Courts.
211. LYONS, REV. JOSEPH HENRY, J.C.L., The Joinder of Issue in Canonical Trials.

www.ingramcontent.com/pod-product-compliance
Lightning Source LLC
LaVergne TN
LVHW050229080826
844660LV00012B/499

* 9 7 8 0 8 1 3 2 2 3 8 2 7 *